Living Water

An Anthology of Letters of Direction

Selected and Introduced by
Robin Baird-Smith

WILLIAM B. EERDMANS PUBLISHING COMPANY
GRAND RAPIDS, MICHIGAN

First published 1987 in Great Britain by Fount Paperbacks,
William Collins Sons & Co. Ltd., London.

This edition published 1988 through special arrangement with
Collins by Wm. B. Eerdmans Publishing Co., 255 Jefferson Ave. SE.
Grand Rapids, MI 49503

Library of Congress Cataloging-in-Publication Data
Living water : an anthology of letters of direction/
selected and introduced by Robin Baird-Smith.
p.   cm.
Includes index.
ISBN 0-8028-0408-X
1. Spiritual life. 2. Christians—Correspondence.
I. Baird-Smith, Robin.
BV4501.2.L596 1988   88-22096
248—dc19   CIP

Beati quorum via integra est
Psalm 119:1

The only thing that is really worth while
is to become God's friend.
St Gregory of Nyssa

Contents

Introduction

All the letters in this collection were written privately; they were sent from one individual to another to offer the recipient advice or spiritual direction, or to impart a little wisdom. None of the letters was written with publication in mind, so their style is direct and spontaneous. This gives the collection a quality and purpose that are quite distinct from, let us say, a book of sermons or public lectures.

The authors span the centuries, from St Paul to the present day. Most of the letters were written before Freud and Jung gave us new insights into the human mind, but they reveal a psychological understanding and an understanding of the human condition which are timeless.

One of the most striking features of these letters is that their authors often seem to have had almost limitless leisure in which to write them; the recipients clearly also had much time to read and digest their contents. It may seem that the letters are over-scrupulous in encouraging self-examination. They will possibly strike many readers as self-indulgent in their attention to the detail of particular thoughts and feelings. Maybe, however, there is an important lesson in this for us. For most people today are in a rush. Contemplatives and the elderly are an exception, but the rest of us are caught in a spiral of haste as we hurry to keep schedules, to catch buses and trains. We are also anxious to communicate and absorb information with increasing speed; letter writing is out of fashion for with improved communications we can meet to talk or use the telephone. At times, perhaps, we also allow ourselves to believe that we can reach God by talking and running faster.

Living Water

These letters are an antidote to our ever-increasing haste. Reading them quietly may help us to slow down and face ourselves honestly. This book could become a companion, to be kept by the reader in a handbag or briefcase, to be read last thing at night or first thing in the morning.

*

The selection of letters is entirely personal. No doubt many who read it will wonder why such and such a letter or author has not been included. Although the letters are varied, I have tended to concentrate quite heavily upon a few writers. This is because they seem to me to be masters of the art of spiritual letter writing. There is no attempt to represent every denomination as a matter of principle, but I hope none the less that the letters will appeal to a wide range of people from all Christian traditions.

*

The letters are arranged in eight sections, set out in the list of contents. There is an index of authors for those who wish to concentrate upon a particular writer.

1

Openness to God and the Self

1. All for God

What I most desire for you is a certain calmness, which recollection, detachment, and love of God alone can give. St Augustine says that whatever we love outside God so much the less do we love Him; it is as a brook whence part of the waters is turned aside. Such a diversion takes away from that which is God's, and thence arise harass and trouble. God would have all, and His jealousy cannot endure a divided heart; the slightest affection apart from Him becomes a hindrance, and causes estrangement. The soul can only look to find peace in love without reserve.

Dissipation,[1] the great foe of recollection, excites all human feelings, distracts the soul, and drives it from its true resting place. Further still, it kindles the senses and imagination; and to quiet them again is a hard task, while the very effort to do so is in itself an inevitable distraction.

Concern yourself as little as possible with external matters. Give a quiet, calm attention to those things assigned to your care by Providence at proper seasons, and be sure that you can accomplish a great deal more by quiet thoughtful work done as in God's sight, than by all the busy eagerness and over-activity of your restless nature.

François Fénelon

---

[1] The sense in which Fénelon uses this word must always be borne in mind, not that in modern use among ourselves, but "a scattering abroad", its original meaning.

2. *The Love of God*

The love of God is by nature pure, balanced and holy. Whoever is dominated by it lives in deep peace, has an ordered view of things and knows the meaning of true freedom. But the love of God, too, passing into man's heart, must be worked at, cultivated, pruned, fertilized. And the most uncompromising farmer is God Himself.

Above all such love must be purified.

What does it mean, to purify love?

It means releasing love from the fetters of the senses and from the pursuit of pleasure. In other words, making it free to grow in our hearts.

Freeing the gift of love! What a difficult undertaking for creatures like ourselves, willingly trapped as we are by sin, shut in by our selfishness.

We often fail to realize the depth of evil, terrifying as it is. I am not speaking only of the selfishness of the wealthy, heaping up riches for themselves, or of those who sacrifice to achieve their self-selected goals. Or of the dictator who breathes in the incense due only to God.

I am speaking of the selfishness of good people, devout people, those who have succeeded through spiritual exercises and self-denial in being able to make the proud profession before the altar of the Most High, "Lord, I am not like the rest of men." Yes, we have had the audacity at certain times of our lives to believe we are different from other men. And here is the deepest form of self-deception, dictated by self-centredness at its worst: spiritual egotism. This most insidious form of egotism even uses piety and prayer for its own gain.

This becomes a form of insult to the altar itself. It is

when the very desire for holiness itself is turned upside down. It is not love and imitation of Christ Crucified, it is the desire for glory. It is not charity, it is egotism.

I believe very strongly that a large proportion of the good intentions which drive us on to seek God are ruined in this way. One can reach the point of consecrating oneself to God for egotistic motives, becoming a religious for that reason, building hospitals, doing all kinds of good works.

There is no limit to such self-deception. And the path, once entered upon, is so slippery that God has to treat us harshly to bring us back to our senses.

But there is no other way of opening our eyes. It has to be painful.

But often it isn't enough. Disaster, illness, disappointment hover like birds of prey over the poor carcass that had the temerity to say, "Lord, I am not like the rest of men."

How can we possibly entertain the idea that we are different from other men, when we shout, cry, feel afraid, lack determination, and behave atrociously just like everybody else?

> Yahweh my God, I call for help all day,
> I weep to you all night;
> for my soul is all troubled,
> my life is on the brink of Sheol;
> I am numbered among those who go down to the pit,
> a man bereft of strength:
> You have plunged me to the bottom of the pit,
> to its darkest, deepest place,
> weighed down by your anger,
> drowned beneath your waves.
>
> (Psalm 88)

It is the purification of love, the refining fire which exposes our nakedness.

And God Himself, who is love, is not powerless.

15

On the contrary, because He is love, He acts with greater determination.

If the soul does not free itself by way of the cross it can never be free. It is the tremendous surgical operation which the Father Himself carries out on the flesh of His Son in order to save Him. And it is a dogma of faith that without the cross "there is no forgiveness". A mystery, but it is so. Pain purifies love. It makes it true, real, pure. And in addition it gets rid of what is not really love. It frees love from pleasure which falsifies it like a mask. It makes it a gift freely given.

When the flood of pain has passed over the soul, what remains alive can be considered genuine. Certainly not much remains. Often it is reduced to a thin shrub. But on this the dove of the Holy Spirit may rest to pour out His grace. It is reduced to a "yes" murmured among tears and anguish, but echoed by the all-powerful "yes" of the dying Jesus; it is reduced to a child who has ceased to argue with God and men, but is helped on by the kiss of the Father.

In this state the soul is capable of a love which is freely given. It can no longer bear any other kind of love. It feels nausea when faced with sentiment. It loathes calculated love. It has finally entered into the logic of God, so often illogical to men of this earth.

Let us consider the logic of the most famous parable on the nature of true love:

The Kingdom of Heaven is like a householder who went out early in the morning to hire labourers for his vineyard. After agreeing with the labourers for a denarius a day, he sent them into his vineyard. And going out about the third hour he saw others standing idle in the market place: and to them he said, "You go into the vineyard too, and whatever is right I will give you." So they went. Going out again about the sixth hour and the ninth hour he did the same. And about the eleventh hour he went out and found others standing; and he said to them, "Why do you stand here idle all day?" They said to him, "Because no one has hired us." He said to them, "You go into the vineyard too." And when evening came the owner said to his steward, "Call the labourers and pay them their wages, beginning with the last, up to the first." And when those hired about the eleventh hour came, each of them received a denarius. Now when the first came, they thought they would receive more; but each of them also received a denarius. And on receiving it they grumbled at the householder, saying, "These last worked only one hour, and you have made them equal to us who have borne the burden of the day and the scorching heat." But he replied to one of them, "Friend, I am doing you no wrong; did you not agree with me for a denarius? Take what belongs to you and go; I chose to give to this last as I give to you. Am I not allowed to do what I choose with what belongs to me? Or is your eye evil because I am good?"

(Matthew 20:1–6)

Understanding this parable for us who have an "evil eye" is not easy. Anyone who understands it just a little before he dies is blessed. For it means that now his eye sees straight and thus he can enter into the kingdom of freedom which is the kingdom of a love which is real and unqualified.

Carlo Carretto

3. *The Motive is Love*

I have received today two books and a letter from Sister —, who is preparing to make her profession, and upon that account desires the prayers of your holy community, and yours in particular . . . I will send you one of these books which treat of the presence of God, a subject which, in my opinion, contains the whole spiritual life: and it seems to me that whoever duly practises it will soon become spiritual.

I know that for the right practice of it the heart must be empty of all else, because God wills to possess the heart alone; and as He cannot possess it alone unless it be empty of all besides, so He cannot work in it what He would unless it be left vacant to Him.

There is not in the world a kind of life more sweet and delightful than that of a continual walk with God.

Those only can comprehend it who practise and experience it; yet I do not advise you to do it from that motive.

It is not pleasure which we ought to seek in this exercise; but let us do it from the motive of love, and because God would have us so walk.

Brother Lawrence

4. Love of God

Spend your time in loving our Lord as simply as possible and without any afterthought, just because He is the ideal and He belongs to you. He is so gentle and humble of heart that it is pure delight to talk to Him quite frankly, without any spiritual tension, in complete simplicity.

*

Never think for a moment of what you are when you contemplate God and our Lord. See Him only as He who is most to be loved and most loving. That thought alone will wipe out all your sins, even though they be great. Love of God is salvation itself, and we love naturally by His grace, because He is the very ideal of that which attracts the heart and the affections. He answers exactly to that which we long to love without measure.

*

What I should like to see springing up in your life would be an easier, more confident, more spontaneous love for Jesus, whom you love so much in reality, but with whom you have not yet learnt to practise an absolutely free and childlike intimacy. If you would only say to yourself that Jesus is absolutely lovable, quite apart from all that you are or are not, and that in consequence you have always the right to love Him in your heart, even if you cannot always succeed in loving Him by acts; then you would be in the Truth. If you would say to yourself firmly that Jesus is unbelievably and unimaginably loving, and that His love does not vary with the variations of your soul, you would be in the Truth. For real affection is never dependent on the fluctuations of those whom it loves; what may vary, according to our feelings and acts, is the satisfaction of our Lord. But we must never confuse "to be satisfied" with "to be loved".

*

In order that this grace may have its full expression and expansion in you, God asks only one thing and that is that you should be on close and friendly terms with Him, without fear; without exception; I was about to say, without ceremony. The fact is that we do not love fully and with our whole being, unless we can be on the same terms with God as we are with our own souls. Then our love is full, true, deep, whole, indestructible, and as it were, instinctive. We lack nothing; we are hampered by nothing; in everything we enjoy the happiness of an absolute intimacy, a complete familiarity.

*

Do not keep accounts with our Lord and say, "I did Him such an injury, therefore He owes me such a grudge. He cannot be on good terms with me because I have not paid Him this or that; it would not be just otherwise."

Go bankrupt! Let our Lord love you without justice! Say frankly, "He loves me because I do not deserve it; that is the wonderful thing about Him; and that is why I, in my turn, love Him as well as I can without worrying whether I deserve to be allowed to love Him. He loves me although I am not worthy; I love Him without being worthy to love."

I know no other way of loving God. Therefore burn your account books! You actually ask me how these two things can go together in human nature, in this nature of ours which is continuously full of contradictions?

You will always offend God in some way; that is only one reason the more for making amends, both to yourself and to Him, by loving Him always and for evermore.

Abbé de Tourville

5. *God Loves Us*

How happy God is in loving us! Like parents who adore their children. It is really just like that and it is *grand*, and just what we should expect of God. It is also necessary for us, poor little creatures that we are. Praise God!

*

Be bold enough always to believe that God is on your side and wholly yours, whatever you may think of yourself.

*

As for that which is beyond your strength, be absolutely certain that our Lord loves you, devotedly and individually: loves you just as you are. How often that conviction is lacking even in those souls who are most devoted to God! They make repeated efforts to love Him, they experience the joy of loving, and yet how little they know, how little they realize, that God loves them incomparably more than they will ever know how to love Him. Think only of this and say to yourself "I am loved by God more than I can either conceive or understand." Let this fill all your soul and all your prayer and never leave you. You will soon see that this is the way to find God. It contains the whole of St John's teaching: "As for us, we have believed in the love which God has for us." I have asked God to teach me this and now I understand it. I know that it is the true way, the best way and the way which is so often lacking in souls. Find it without delay.

Accustom yourself to the wonderful thought that God loves you with a tenderness, a generosity, and an intimacy which surpasses all your dreams. Give yourself up with joy to a loving confidence in God and have courage to believe firmly that God's action towards you is a masterpiece of partiality and love. Rest tranquilly in this abiding conviction.

*

The thing which may for long prevent the soul from thus accepting our Lord, is that it forgets to think of Him always and above all as compassionate. Yet in everything, that is the first idea we must try to have about Him. We shall be quite differently affected by His great splendour if we first realize that He to whom it belongs and who offers it to us, is compassionate beyond all words. How gladly shall we then rejoice in His divine splendours! For they are the splendours of the All-Compassionate, the Intimate, and the Familiar God!

*

We must think of our Lord as loving us more than any one else, upholding us even when we are ready mercilessly to condemn ourselves; think of Him as being our other self, bolder in approval and more ready to rejoice over us than we are ourselves. That is the ideal of fatherhood, of friendship and of love. When we know our Lord thus, we know Him well and everything is easy. The terrible God, the angry, exacting, narrow God, has completely disappeared. We are attracted to our Lord and profoundly reassured. And so we love with confidence and joy.

Rejoice that you are what you are; for our Lord loves you very dearly. He loves the whole of you, just as you are. In spite therefore of all your troubles, troubles about people and things, remain at peace. Drop all your spiritual anxieties and do not goad yourself to efforts which will only overburden and overstrain you. Such efforts are not only useless but even harmful, for they war against that peace which the Christ-God demands: the peace which, in this world, must always exist in the midst of our imperfections: the imperfections of things, the imperfections of people. Imitate the calm of the sailor standing on the deck of his ship, which is in itself never still: or that of the man who walks quietly through the city, indifferent to the noise and the winding of the streets, picking his way through the people and the traffic . . .

Be reassured and comforted. Rejoice from the bottom of your heart at this assurance I am giving you, as if it came from our Lord Himself. For it is only in this blessed certitude that you will find that freedom of spirit which is absolutely necessary. I implore you in God's name, not to think of Him as hard to please, but rather as generous beyond all that you can ask or think. Get rid, once and for all, of the idea that God is displeased or intolerant towards our weakness. The truth is exactly the opposite. Accept that fact and act upon it.

*

You have not grasped the right idea of God and of His service. You always come back to the thought that God must be dissatisfied, which is not so. Remember that it is our souls, yes! our own souls! which are God's joy: not on account of what He does for them. All that He asks of them is gladly to accept His kindness, His generosity, His tolerance, His fatherly love. Let your adoration of God, therefore, take this form and do not worry any more about what you are or are not. You are the object of His mercy. Be satisfied with that and think only of that.

*

The essence of the matter is that our Lord loves you dearly. The more keenly, therefore, you realize that the weakness is of your own nature, even of your own will, the more you must adore Him. For in spite of everything, we *are* the weak creatures whom our Lord loves, and loves deeply, with a love worthy of that name, which to Him is no idle word.

You want to compete with His affection before you have understood it; that is your mistake. You are like a child who wants to help his mother before allowing himself to be trained by her. You are like St Peter; he wanted to wash his Master's feet, but refused to allow his Master to wash his feet. He did not understand. Our Lord showed him his mistake with the clear and decisive sharpness of a friend: "Peter! if I do not do this, and if you will not let me do it, you have no part in me!" And St John, who knew all the depth and tenderness of God's love, was constantly ravished by the thought, "He loved us first!"

Come then! show a little deference to our Lord and allow Him to go first. Let Him love you a great deal, a very great deal, long before you have succeeded in loving Him, even a little, as you would wish to love Him.

That is all I ask of you, and all that our Lord asks of you.

*

Say to yourself very often about everything that happens, "God loves me! What a joy!" And reply boldly, "And I truly love Him too!" Then go quite simply about all that you have to do and do not philosophize any more. For these two phrases are beyond all thought and do more for us than any thought could do; they are all-sufficing.

Abbé de Tourville

6. *Christian Perfection*

Christian perfection is not the strict, wearisome, constrained thing you suppose. It requires a person to give himself to God with his whole heart, and so soon as this is accomplished, whatever he is called upon to do for God becomes easy. Those who are wholly God's are always satisfied, for they desire only that which He wills, and are ready to do whatever He requires; they are ready to strip themselves of all things, and are sure to find a hundredfold in that nakedness. This hundredfold happiness which the true children of God possess amid all the troubles of this world consists in a peaceful conscience, freedom of spirit, a welcome resignation of all things to God, the joyful sense of His light ever waxing stronger within their heart, and a thorough deliverance from all tyrannous fears and longings after worldly things. They make sacrifices, but for Him they love best; they suffer, but willingly, and realizing such suffering to be better than any worldly joy; their body may be diseased, their mind languid and shrinking, but their will is firm and steadfast, and they can say a hearty *Amen* to every blow which it pleases God to deal them.

What God requires is an undivided will – a yielding will, desiring only what He desires, rejecting only what He rejects, and both unreservedly. Where such a mind is everything turns to good, and its very amusements become good works. Happy indeed is such a one! he is delivered from all his own passions – from the judgements of men, their unkindness, their slavish maxims, their cold, heartless mockery; from the troubles of what the world calls fortune; from the treachery or forgetfulness of friends, the snares of enemies, his own weakness; from the weariness of this brief life, the terrors of an unholy death, the bitter remorse which follows sin, and from the eternal condemnation of God. From all these endless evils the Christian is set free; he has resigned his will to God and knows no will save His, and thus faith and hope are his comfort amid all possible sorrows. Is it not a grievous mistake to be afraid to give yourself to God and to commit yourself to so blessed a state of things? Blessed are they who throw themselves headlong and blindfold into the arms of "the Father of all mercies and God of all comfort" (2 Corinthians 1:3).

Nothing remains for them save to know Him better and better; no fear, save lest they be not quick enough to see what He requires. Directly that they discover any fresh light from His Law, they "rejoice as one that findeth a hid treasure". Let what may befall the true Christian, all is well to his mind; he only seeks to love God more, and the further he learns to tread in the way of perfection the lighter he feels his yoke.

Cannot you see that it is mere folly to be afraid of giving yourself too entirely to God? It merely means that you are afraid of being too happy, of accepting His Will in all things too heartily, of bearing your inevitable trials too bravely, of finding too much rest in His love, and of sitting too loosely to the worldly passions which make you miserable. Try to despise all that is of the world that you may be wholly God's. I do not say that you should cut yourself off from all earthly affections; to one like yourself, who is leading a good, well-regulated life, all that is needed is that the motive power become that of love. You would then do very much the same things that you do now, for God does

26

not alter the condition He has assigned to each or the duties appertaining thereto: the alteration would be that, whereas now you fulfil your duties for your own satisfaction and that of the world around, you would then pursue the same line as now; but instead of being eaten up by pride or passion – instead of living in bondage to the world's malicious criticism – you would act freely and bravely in the fulness of hope in God – you would be full of trust, and looking forward to eternal blessings would comfort you for the earthly happiness which seems to slip from under your feet; God's love would give wings to your feet in treading His paths and lifting you up beyond all your cares. If you doubt me, try: "O taste and see how gracious the Lord is!"

The Son of God says to all Christians without any exception, "If any man will come after Me, let him take up his cross and follow Me" (Matthew 16:24). The broad road leads to destruction; strive to follow that narrow path on which so few enter. Only the "violent take the Kingdom of Heaven by storm". You must be born anew, renounce and despise yourself, become as a little child, mourn that you may be comforted, and not be of this world, which is condemned because of unbelief.

These truths frighten many, and that because they only see what religion requires without realizing what it offers, or the loving spirit by which it makes every burthen light. They do not understand that such religion leads a person to the very highest perfection by filling him with a loving peace which lightens every woe. Those who have given themselves unreservedly to God are always happy. They realize that the yoke of Jesus Christ is light and easy, that in Him they do indeed find rest, and that He lightens the load of all that are weary and heavy laden, as He promised. But what can be more wretched than those hesitating, cowardly souls which are divided between God and the world. They will and will not; they are torn asunder both by their own passions and by remorse at their indulgence; they are alike afraid of God's judgements and those of men; they are afraid of what is evil and ashamed of what is good; they have all the trials of goodness without its comfort! If they had but the courage to despise idle talk, petty ridicule, and the rash judgements of men, what peace and rest they might enjoy in the bosom of God!

Nothing is more perilous to your own salvation, more unworthy of God, or more hurtful to your ordinary happiness, than being content to abide as you are. Our whole life is given us with the object of going boldly on towards the heavenly home. The world slips away like a deceitful shadow, and eternity draws near; why delay to push forward? While it is time, while your Merciful Father lights up your path, make haste and seek His Kingdom.

The first Commandment of the Law alone is enough to banish all excuse for any reserve with God: "Thou shalt love the Lord thy God with all thy heart, and with all thy soul, and with all thy strength, and with all thy mind" (Luke 10:27). Observe how our Lord heaped together expressions which would forestall all the soul's evasions and reservations as regards God's jealous love, requiring not merely the heart's strength and power, but that of the mind and thought. Who can deceive himself by thinking he loves God if he does not willingly ponder His Law, or try diligently to fulfil His holy will? Be sure that all those who are reluctant to perceive fully what His love requires are yet a long way off from it. There is but one true way of loving God, i.e. to do nothing save with and for Him, and to obey His every call with a "free spirit". Those who aim at a compromise, who would fain hold on to the world with one hand, cannot believe this, and so they run the risk of being among those "lukewarm" whom God will reject (Revelation 3:16).

Surely those cowardly souls which say, "Thus far will I go, but no farther", must be most displeasing to God. Does it beseem the clay to dictate to the potter? What would men of the world think of a servant or a subject who presumed to offer such a half-service to his master or monarch, who shrank from a too hearty fulfilment of his duty, and was ashamed to let his loyalty be seen? And if so, what will the King of Kings say if we pursue such cowardly conduct? The time is at hand, He will soon come; let us prevent Him, let us adore that eternal beauty which never grows old, and which imparts perpetual youth to such as love none else. Let us turn from this miserable world, which is already beginning to crumble away. How many great people we have lately seen pass away beneath the cold hand of Death! We shall soon be called to leave this world we love so dearly, and which is nought save vanity, weakness, and folly – a mere shadow passing away.

François Fénelon

7. *Making the Choice*

3 August 1851

You are now of an age to choose your future career; an age when people begin to think for themselves, and when certain convictions are formed in the mind and influence the conduct. In your intercourse with men, you will encounter much prejudice, many strange ideas and perversions of the truth, for society in Europe has become thoroughly corrupt. I do not mean to say that there were not plenty of bad people in olden times just as there are now, for man is ever the same. But formerly there were certain social canons and conventions that none but the really profligate disregarded. Religion was the accepted foundation of society, and God gives life to nations as well as to individuals. Now all these safeguards are removed or ignored, as you will realize when you grow older.

Well, you are wondering about your future. Pray simply, humbly, and fervently to know God's will, and your path will be made clear. Then you must follow the inspiration divine Mercy puts into your heart. Some say: "I will be a priest", or "a soldier", and they add: "Oh, such and such studies are not necessary for this or that professional." This is the reasoning of pure idlers. Others go on about piety: "Piety! It's only for priests and nuns. God does not expect so much from us!" (*How do you know?*) These are the arguments of cold and calculating natures. Now I want you to say to yourself: "I am, above all, a man, a rational being, created to know, love, serve, and glorify God. I come from God. I go to God. I belong to God. My body is His. My mind is His. My heart is His. I shall be judged according to my deeds, according to the way I have corresponded with the grace given me. Well, then, by God's help, I shall use this body, this mind, and this heart as much as I possibly can for His greater glory, honour and love." Life well employed consists in this: A faithful correspondence to grace and a good use of the talents we have been given. This rule of life applies equally to all.

But you want to know, "What does God ask of *me*?" Humility, prayer, obedience to His divine commands and to the voice of our mother the Church, and complete self-surrender to His divine providence. You tell me that your hopes, your tastes, the secret inspiration of grace draw you strongly towards the priesthood. May God's holy name be praised! If our Lord calls you, you must respond. One day the child Samuel heard a voice crying aloud, "Samuel, Samuel!" "Here I am, Lord", he replied. If you think our Lord has called you, then like Samuel you must answer: "Here I am, Lord. What wilt Thou have me to do? With the help of Thy grace, I will do all Thou dost appoint, for I know that grace will never be withheld." You are the child of our divine Lord and His blessed Mother, the child of His love, the sheep of His pasture; have confidence in God. Never forget that God is in everything, little as well as great. He ought to be the one motive of your thoughts, words and actions. A great future stretches before you, a high vocation. Anchored on God's infinite mercy, repeat humbly yet with complete trust the words of St Paul: *I press on towards the goal, to the prize of God's heavenly call in Christ Jesus* (Philippians 3:14). O Eusebius, you are at the grandest moment of your life! Shall I tell you why? Because you are at an age of strong passions, of hard struggles, of mighty victories. Our Lord "looks" upon a young man and "loves" him. That young man is yourself. Courage, be worthy of your Master! Perhaps you and I shall find ourselves soldiers of the same regiment, travellers on the same road, bound for the same destination. May His holy will, not ours, be done! Leave your future in His hands, in the heart of Jesus made man. Remember that He too was once a young man, for Jesus Christ is the God-child, the God-youth, the God-man, the God of all ages.

Try to fulfil each day's task steadily and cheerfully. Be merry, really merry. The life of a true Christian should be a perpetual jubilee, a prelude to the festivals of eternity. I am going to ask you to do one thing for me. For a few mintues every day, read and meditate upon one or two verses of St John's Gospel, chapters 14–17. That is our Lord's parting sermon to man, and every letter is a precious pearl. Pray daily in the words of Solomon for wisdom and understanding: "God of my fathers and Lord of mercy, who hast made all things with Thy word, give me wisdom that sitteth by Thy throne. For I am Thy servant and the son of Thy handmaid, a weak man of few days upon the earth, and falling short of the understanding of judgement. Send wisdom out of Thy holy heaven that she may be with me and labour with me, that I may know what is acceptable before Thee – and do it. Amen."

Blessed Théophane Vénard
to his brother Eusebius

2

Self-Abandonment to God

1. The First Work of God in the Soul

1731

I am not at all surprised at the first effect of your meditating on the great truths; I congratulate you and give thanks to the Lord. You were in need of these acute feelings, and I believe that they will last so as to produce in you that spirit of compunction and humiliation which should be the foundation of your spiritual edifice and the commencement of your spiritual childhood. The agitation accompanying these feelings was superfluous, but, unless I am mistaken, it was involuntary and perhaps necessary and an effect of divine justice. These same feelings, when they return, will in future be gentler and more peaceful.

I had already understood, independently of your letter, that God had bestowed great graces on you; I had already divined that you had not corresponded sufficiently with them and I understand more clearly than ever:

1. That your soul is like a great hall, unfurnished or insufficiently furnished.
2. That it will never be fit for the reception of our sovereign Lord unless He Himself furnishes it and arranges in it the precious furniture suitable for such a guest.
3. That the only way in which He will do this and enrich your soul with His gifts will be during the silence and peace of prayer.

Your duty is, therefore, to keep the hall well swept and clean with the help of grace, and, then, give place to Him who will make it His own business to supply the beautiful furniture with which it is to be enriched, and who wishes to arrange it according to His own taste.

Do not go and upset yourself for nothing in a matter in which you would spoil everything by interference. Let him do as He likes; consider yourself as a picture which a great master is proposing to paint; but take courage, for I foresee that it will take some time to grind and powder the colours, and then to lay them on, combine them and shade them. All you have to do is to keep the canvas ready, well-cleaned and fastened on its two motionless pivots, the one being self-humiliation pushed to the point of self-annihilation, the other a complete self-abandonment pushed to the point of losing your will altogether in the will of God.

Jean-Pierre de Caussade
to Madame de Lesen

2. *The Virtue of Self-Abandonment*

Albi, 1733

You are quite right in what you say, my dear daughter, and indeed the great maxim of Blessed Mother de Chantal was: "Not so many opinions, so much learning and writing, but sound practice." As regards souls which have acquired the habit of avoiding deliberate faults and faithfully fulfilling the duties of their state of life, all practical perfection may be reduced to this one principle: the exercise of a continual resignation to all the manifestations of the will of God, a complete self-abandonment to all the exterior or interior dispositions of His Providence, whether in the present or in the future; one single *fiat*, or in St Francis de Sales' words:

"Yes, heavenly Father, I accept everything; yes, and always yes." This phrase said and repeated, without its being necessary that it should be pronounced interiorly, represents in a few words the great and short road of the highest perfection because it tells of a continual union with the holy and adorable will of God.

There is no mystery about the way to reach that point; only two things are necessary: firstly, the profound conviction that nothing happens in this world, in our souls or outside them, without the design or permission of God; now, we ought to submit ourselves no less to what God permits than to what He directly wills; secondly, the firm belief that through the all-powerful and paternal Providence of God, all that He wills or permits invariably turns to the advantage of those who practise this submission to His orders. Supported by this double assurance, let us remain firm and unshakeable in our adhesion to all that it may please God to ordain with regard to us, let us acquiesce in advance, in a spirit of humility, love and sacrifice in all imaginable dispositions of His Providence, let us protest that we wish to be content with whatever satisfies Him. We shall not always be able, no doubt, to feel this contentment in the lower (the sensitive) part of our soul, but we shall at least preserve it on the heights of our spirit, on the fine point of our will, as St Francis de Sales says, and in those circumstances it will be even more meritorious.

Jean-Pierre de Caussade
to Sister Marie Henriette de Bousmard

3. The Love of God

What do I think I am doing, my dear daughter, writing you these little letters of mine to give comfort to your heart, when you can derive much better and more enjoyable comfort from taking and reading that book of life, that scroll of the perfect law which converts our souls, which you have daily before your mind's eye? That law which is perfect, because it takes away all imperfections, is charity, and you find it written with strange beauty when you gaze at Jesus your Saviour stretched out like a sheet of parchment on the cross, inscribed with wounds, illustrated in His own loving blood. Where else, I ask you, my dearest, is there a comparable book of love to read from? You know better than I do, that no letter could inspire love more passionately. So fix your mind's attention there. Hide in the clefts of this rock, hide yourself away from the clamour of those who speak wickedness. Turn this book over, open it, read it; you will find in it what the prophet found: lamentations, song and woe. Lamentations, because of the pains which He endured; a song of gladness, which He won for you by His pains; and the woe of unending death, from which He redeemed you by His death. In His lamentations, learn to have patience in yourself, learn love in His song of joy, because surely He has the first claim on your love, seeing that He wanted you to be a sharer in such great joys. And when you realize that you have been rescued from that woe, what else should result but thanksgiving and the sound of praise? These are short words, but to a loving heart they are long and deep

38

enough. I want you, my daughter, to accustom yourself to dwelling in these words, and to learn the wisdom of the saints, as you are taught and stirred and guided by the Son of God, Jesus Christ, to whom be honour and glory forever. Amen.

Farewell in Christ Jesus. Greet everybody for me whom you know I would want to greet.

Brother Jordan O.P.
to a Nun, Sister Diana

4. *Poor in Spirit*

No cask can hold two different kinds of drink. If it is to contain wine, then they must of necessity pour the water out; the cask must become empty and free. Therefore, if you are to receive God's joy and God, you are obliged to pour out created things. St Augustine says: "Empty yourself, so that you may be filled. Learn not to love, so that you may learn how to love. Draw back, so that you may be approached." In a few words, everything that is to receive and be capable of receiving should and must be empty. The authorities say that if the eye had some colour in it when it was observing, it would recognize neither the colour it had nor the colour it had not; but because it is free of all colours, it therefore recognizes all colours. A wall has its own colour, and therefore it recognizes neither its colour nor any other colour, and it takes no pleasure in colours, no more in that of gold or lapis lazuli than in that of charcoal. The eye has no colour and yet truly possesses colour, because it recognizes it with pleasure and delight and joy. And as the powers of the soul become more perfect and unmixed, so they apprehend more perfectly and comprehensively whatever they apprehend, receiving it more comprehensively, having greater joy, becoming more united with what they apprehend, to the point where the highest power of the soul, bare of all things and having nothing in common with anything, receives into itself nothing less than God Himself, in all the vastness and fulness of His being. And the authorities show us that there is no delight and no joy that can be compared with this union and this fulfilling and this joy. This is why our Lord says so insistently: "Blessed are the poor in spirit" (Matthew 5:3). A man is poor who has nothing. To be poor in spirit means that as the eye is poor and deprived of colour, and is able to apprehend every colour, so he is poor in spirit who is able to apprehend every spirit, and the Spirit of all spirits is God. The fruit of the spirit is love, joy and peace (Galatians 5:22). To be naked, to be poor, to have nothing, to be empty transforms nature; emptiness makes water flow uphill, and many other marvels of which we need not now speak.

Therefore, if you want to have and to find complete joy and consolation in God, make sure that you are naked of all created things, of all comfort from created things; for truly, so long as created things console you and can console you, never will you find true consolation. But when nothing but God can console you, then truly God does console you, and with Him and in Him everything that is joy consoles you. If what is not God consoles you, then you will have no consolation, neither now nor later. But if creatures do not console you and give you no delight, then you will find consolation, both now and to come.

If a man were able and knew how to make a goblet quite empty, and to keep it empty of everything that could fill it, even of air, doubtless the goblet would forgo and forget all its nature, and its emptiness would lift it up into the sky. And so to be naked, poor, empty of all created things lifts the soul up to God. Likeness and heat too draw up above. We attribute likeness in the divinity to the Son, heat and love to the Holy Spirit. Likeness in all things, but more so and first of all in the divine nature, is the birth of the One and the likeness of the One, in the One and with the One; it is the beginning and origin of flowering, fiery love. The One is the beginning without any beginning. Likeness is the beginning of the One alone, and it receives that it is and that it is beginning from the One and in the One. It is the nature of love that it flows and springs up out of two as one. One as one does not produce love, two as two does not produce love; two as one perforce produces natural, consenting, fiery love.

Meister Eckhart

5. *Confidence in God*

Above everything else you must develop confidence in the love which our Lord bears you. That must become your chief virtue. Consequently you must practise gratitude, tranquillity, joy, and affection; and this most of all when things are not going well with you, when something sinful and warped gets hold of you. Because it is just then that we most need to remember this love which does not forsake us, but calls us back.

*

If you base your confidence in God on the thought that He loves you on account of your merits, then your confidence in Him will always be very feeble. But once you base your confidence and certitude of being loved on the free and permanent and incessant gift of grace, then your confidence will be sure and strong.

*

When bit by bit you have given up scrutinizing your soul and the Christian life according to a mass of petty theological rules; when you have simply thrown yourself at the feet of our Lord, following the impulse of your particular nature and grace; when you have done this tranquilly, without strain and without afterthought, sure of that which is most real – *then* you will have made a great step forward and truly found God.

Let us go to Him who is goodness itself with a simplicity full of confidence. I beg you to banish all fear, all apprehension and to incline to nothing but peace, frankness, and joy. Love our Lord tranquilly in the knowledge that He is infinitely lovable; that is all. After that it is for Him to take charge of us, and He will not be found wanting.

*

What ought to make us most afraid is our weakness, our cowardice, our detestable nature; but we escape this fear precisely by casting ourselves on our Lord, relying on Him to save us, in spite of everything.

*

I order, I command, I beg, I insist, I entreat you to lay aside all fear of God. It is ridiculous. You do not understand what God is like. He is the most sympathetic of friends, always biased in our favour, always most indulgent, most generous. Everything which has represented God to you as other than this, is a legacy from Judaism and paganism. What fear have you of the Judgement? Would you like to to be judged by me at the Gates of Heaven? Would you feel confident that I should be lenient? Of course you would! Very well then! God will be more lenient still, because He is better than I am, and loves you, as is His right, in a still more fatherly way. This is absolutely true and you must change your ideas about this completely. You must feel nothing but confidence in the infinite mercy of God.

*

I tell you as solemnly as if our Lord said it Himself, that you must cease to have any fear of Him, for fear grieves Him. When you are in any trouble; even if, alas! you have brought it on yourself, throw yourself boldly at the feet of our Saviour, at the feet of rescuing Love; hide yourself in this sanctuary and be so ravished by God's gentleness and tenderness, that you come to love and know Him a little better. This is what He asks of you, and this is the result He means your difficulties to produce in you. You will afterwards imitate His compassion as well as you can towards others, thus modelling yourself, your heart and soul, on Jesus Christ, becoming His true ministering servant.

*

The wonderful works of God are not always revealed to us. It is through events that they are revealed and we may be sure of the results. This is what is called the test of fidelity.

*

Our Lord watches over His own. Those who seek Him always find, under one form or another, all that they need for the wise guidance of their souls. It is above all in this form of blessing that God manifests Himself.

I have constantly experienced that in my own case, in the most diverse and unforeseen circumstances. I have always found our Lord providing in the nick of time, that which is best for the training of the soul. Always have absolute confidence in this for the Gospel proclaims it: "I am the Good Shepherd; my sheep hear my voice. I lead them! I know them each by name and they follow Me!"

As soon as we become observant we see at once that our Lord is our true and chief director, who, without our knowledge, has arranged matters in such a way that our lives turn out quite differently from what we should have expected; infinitely better for our salvation and glory than we should ever have dared hope.

*

God gradually takes away our supports, whether of nature or of grace. With the passing of time we are apt to become aware of the menace of finding ourselves left alone. What resource do you suppose there is, save that of making up our minds to put ourselves completely and delightedly into the hands of God? That is what we must do, casting a glance of absolute confidence towards Him: a confidence founded solely on His goodness. Do not argue with Him. Tell Him frankly that all your fears will not frighten, nor all your unworthiness intimidate you, when it comes to trusting Him; that in spite of everything, you do trust Him and, moreover, with peace, serenity, and love, both in season and out of season.

Abbé de Tourville

6. *Offering Your Being to God*

The path to this spiritual consciousness is the one I have recommended, together with the help of the grace that knows in advance what you really require. The path, then, demands that you constantly insist on bare consciousness of your own self, always offering your being – the most valuable sacrifice you can offer – to God. But you must be careful, as I have always said, that your consciousness of self is bare and unadorned, unless you want to be taken in. If it is a bare and unadorned awareness of self, it will of course cause you a lot of anguish initially to be with it for more than a moment. This, as I have already told you, is because your natural abilities can't find anything worthwhile for themselves in that kind of awareness. But that doesn't matter in the least – on the contrary, it's all the better if for a time you allow your natural faculties to go without the natural enjoyment of knowing. Of course it is right to say that a human being naturally wants to know, but it is also true to say no one can experience God – tasting Him in spirit, that is – by any means other than grace, no matter how much natural or acquired knowledge he or she possesses. That is why I advise you to look for experience rather than for knowledge. Knowing often misleads us because of our pride, but mere awareness in love and humility is without deceit. As we read in Corinthians, knowing demands work, experience gives rest.

Of course you are bound to ask what kind of rest St Paul and I refer to, for you will think that it isn't peaceful at all, but just labour – and hard, painful labour at that. When you try to do what I recommend, all you seem to get is anguish and trouble everywhere. On the one hand, your natural faculties want you to give it all up, but you yourself don't want to; and on the other hand, you want to feel God and to leave your consciousness of self, and yet you can't do so. And so you experience anguish and difficulties in every respect. I can hear you saying: "I find this rest you speak of a very odd variety indeed." My answer to these objections is that you find the exercise distressing because you're not used to it. If you had practised it a lot, and experience had taught you how much you could gain from it, you would not willingly give it up for all the earthly pleasures and peacefulness this world can afford. All the same it is very, very difficult and laborious. Yet I cannot call it anything but rest. The soul is absolutely sure about what it has to do, and while you're practising the exercise, your soul is quite convinced that it can't go far astray.

So proceed with your exercise humbly and ardently. Remember that it is an exercise which begins in this life and will never come to an end in the life everlasting. May Jesus, whose power is infinite, help to the same eternal life all those whom He has bought with His precious blood. Amen.

The Author of
The Cloud of Unknowing

7. *Forgetting One's Own Being*

You may rest assured that although I advise you to forget everything but the blind consciousness of your very being, I want you to, and have intended from the start that you should, forget the consciousness of your own being in the awareness of God's being. And so I proved to you at the beginning that God is your being. Nevertheless, because I thought that you weren't ready yet to be suddenly raised up to spiritual consciousness of God's being, and because you hadn't enough experience of spiritual things, in order to help you to ascend to it gradually, I advised you to practise the blind contemplation of the essence of your very being until you were prepared, through spiritual labour at this secret exercise, to reach that high consciousness of God. Your goal and wish in this exercise must always be to find God. Now, at the start, because you are so rough as yet and haven't enough spiritual experience, I advise you to wrap and cover your consciousness of your God in consciousness of your own self. Later, however, when you have persevered and have become wiser in purity of spirit, you must take off, discard and entirely get rid of every trace of self-awareness, so that you can put on the consciousness of God's very own self, which will bring you grace.

That is how perfect lovers act. They quite rid themselves of their very own selves in order to possess what they love, and won't be dressed in anything other than whatever they love, not just for a short time, but for ever, in full and absolute self-forgetting. Only those who have experienced it can know what it is like to make love in that way. That is what Jesus means when He says: "If people love me, they have to abandon themselves", as if He said: "Let them get rid of themselves if they really want to be clothed in me, for I am the full garment of love that lasts for ever and never shall come to an end."

So when you think about your spiritual exercise and realize that you experience your very self, not God, you must be truly sorry, and desire consciousness of God with all your heart. You must always and incessantly desire to be without this wretched knowing and the awful feeling of your own unseeing being. You must long to get away from yourself as you would from poison. At that point you leave yourself and despise yourself most severely, as Jesus requires. And then when you want so very seriously, not to cease being at all (for that would be madness and despising God), but to get rid of knowing and being conscious of your own being (which must always happen before you can experience God's love as absolutely as one can on this earth), you will truly see and realize that it is quite impossible to reach your goal. The reason that you can't get to it is that no matter how hard you work at it, your actions will always be accompanied by a naked sensation of your unseeing being. (Of course God may exceptionally and briefly allow you to experience Him in the abundance of love – but exceptionally, and briefly.)

This bare feeling of your own unseeing being will continually press above you, between you and your God, as when you start the characteristics of your being press between you and your self. Then your self will seem a very painful and heavy burden to bear. May Jesus come to your aid then, for that is when you need Him. No sorrow of all sorrows in the world can compare with that. Then you are your own cross. This is the true exercise and the way that leads to Jesus, as He says Himself: "Carry your cross" first, or the anguish and burden of self, and then "follow Me to joy, to the heights of perfection, tasting My sweet love and the godlike experience of My self". I am sure that you will be aware at this point how much you need such sorrowful desire to cast down the weight of the self as a cross, before you can be united with God in spiritual consciousness of God Himself, who is perfect love. And so you can see and to some degree realize why this is a finer exercise than any other, to the extent that you are touched spiritually and marked with this grace.

The Author of
The Cloud of Unknowing

8. *Self-Abandonment in Different States of Soul*

1735

My Dear Sister,
    The peace of our Lord Jesus Christ! If we are attentive and docile to the interior spirit, we shall be so surely guarded that we shall rarely make a false step. I approve, however, the wise precaution of sometimes explaining one's state to the ministers of Jesus Christ, through a holy

distrust of oneself. God has so blessed such humility in you that I feel almost inclined to reply to you in one word: All is well, continue. Nevertheless, for your consolation I shall add what God inspires me to add as I re-read your letter.

"I do not care", you say, " to talk or write or read much." What a beautiful confession! It alone indicates a soul which is ordinarily well occupied within itself; a great spiritual writer has said of such persons that they have immense occupations without labour. Another calls this happy disposition by the name of holy leisure or holy unemployment, for it seems that doing nothing means doing all things, and saying nothing, saying everything.

1. I find nothing but good in the three dispositions of soul which you experience in turn: firstly, your disposition of faith, secondly, the disposition of your tastes and sentiments, thirdly, your disposition in the midst of disturbances and troubles; but the degrees of their goodness are different. The first is the simplest and surest, and favours self-love least. The second is more agreeable and demands a great detachment from all personal tastes and feelings, even divine, so as to attach yourself to God purely and solely, as Fénelon says. The third is painful and often excruciating, but it is also the best, because all that mortifies the soul makes it purer and disposes it for a closer union with the God of all purity and holiness.

2. Thanks to His goodness, you behave very well in all these three dispositions of soul; you have only to go on as you are doing, but you explain yourself in a way that would distress those without experience of this state of prayer. You say that you do nothing, and yet you are always doing something or you would be in a state of pure idleness; but your soul acts so gently that you do not perceive your interior acts of consent and adherence to the inspirations of the Holy Spirit. The stronger these inspirations are, the less you should act; you should merely follow what is drawing you and allow yourself to be drawn gently on, as you rightly say.

3. Your manner of behaving in times of storm and upset enchants me. Submission, total self-abandonment without reserve, being content with lack of contentment when God wills it. In those conditions one advances more in one day than in a hundred filled with sweetness and consolations. O my good God! This is indeed the right and solid line to take. Teach it to every one and repeat it often to poor Sister N. Properly speaking, this is all she needs at present: the constant practice of this maxim would make a saint of her and sweeten all her interior sufferings; a little more and with the practice of this point alone, you would see her shortly quite different, as if she had been made over again and transformed.

4. Your total, continual and universal self-abandonment to God through a sentiment of confidence and union with Jesus Christ, always doing the will of His Father, is the most divine and surest method of success in everything; try to communicate it to every one, particularly to the dear Sister of whom I have just spoken.

5. The grace and the light which make you fight and smother the feelings of nature on all the occasions of which you speak deserve to be carefully preserved. Your attention and fidelity in corresponding with these graces, even on the most trifling occasions, are able to increase them still more; but do not wish ever to be delivered from your sensitiveness to your first impulses; they are useful for the preservation of interior humility which is the foundation and guardian of all virtues.

6. As for your habitual faults, you should know that from the moment that our imperfections sincerely displease us and that we are sincerely resolved to combat them without reserve, there is no affection towards them in our heart and consequently nothing that can oppose our union with God. What we have to do then is first of all to work with all our strength at diminishing the number of these faults and imperfections, and when we fall into them by

frailty, surprise or otherwise, to rise immediately with courage and to return to God with the same confidence as if nothing had happened, after having humbled ourselves in His presence and begged His pardon, without any spite against ourselves, or trouble or disquiet. In such a case humility supplies for the lack of fidelity and often repairs our fault with advantage to ourselves. Finally, if there is some little reparation to be made to our neighbour, let us never fail in this duty, but take the opportunity to conquer generously our pride and human respect.

7. When you experience involuntary disorderly impulses, give yourself time, before grace extinguishes them, to realize clearly to what excesses pride and passion would carry you without its help. In this way, you will be able to acquire by personal experience the complete knowledge of that depth of perversity into which we should fall, if God did not keep us back. It is by this practical knowledge, these reiterated feelings, these frequent personal experiences that all the saints have acquired that profound humility of heart, that complete contempt and holy hatred of themselves of which we find so many proofs in the history of their lives and which were the most solid supports of their perfection.

8. As for the feeling of external trouble and temptation, all that you tell me shows me that the Holy Spirit has in this respect regulated so well your thoughts, your feelings, your interior and exterior behaviour, that I have nothing to add. Evidently, if it is certain that the unsought signs of esteem and friendship which we receive are a cross to us instead of a matter of complacency, the distress and disgust that they cause us is an antidote to their poison. There can be nothing but great merit in suffering patiently in conformity with the orders of God and the arrangements of Providence, and in accordance with the example of Jesus Christ, suspicions, false judgements, envy and jealousy without explaining matters or defending oneself further

than is required for the edification of our neighbour. If when we see ourselves exposed to various criticisms and unjust prejudices, we persevere in our line of conduct without change, following the guidance of Providence step by step, we are truly living by faith alone, with God alone in the midst of the quarrels and confusion of creatures. In such a disposition of soul, external things cannot reach our interior life, and the peace which we enjoy can be troubled neither by their favours nor their contempt. This is what is called living the interior life, and a very interior life it is. Until this independence of soul has been acquired the most apparently brilliant virtues are in reality very fragile, superficial and liable to corruption by self-love, or to be upset by the slightest breath of inconstancy and contradiction.

9. Be well on your guard against all illusions, which however specious they may be incline you to follow your own ideas and prefer yourself before others. A self-sufficient and critical spirit seems to many but a trifle, but we cannot deny that such a spirit is greatly opposed to religious simplicity and that it prevents many souls from entering on the interior life. For, indeed, we cannot enter the path of that life unless the Holy Spirit who never gives Himself save to the humble-minded and the simple, introduce us to it.

10. Your profound, delicate, simple and almost imperceptible method of resisting all sorts of temptations is a pure grace of God; attempt no other. That simple turning to God is worth infinitely more than all other kinds of acts. It cannot very well be explained, God alone teaches it and gives it to the soul in the school of the Holy Spirit, which is carried on in the depths of the heart. The peaceful doubts that we experience after temptation are the fruit of chaste fear which should never be eliminated; as for the restless sort of doubt which is born of self-love it should be expelled and despised.

Moreover, nothing in the world is easier to recognize

and uncover than the abuses and illusions to which the prayer of faith and simple recollection is liable; we have but to apply the infallible test of Jesus Christ: the tree is known by its fruits. All prayer, then, which produces reformation of the heart and of conduct, flight from vice, the practice of the evangelical virtues and the duties of one's state, is a good prayer. Contrariwise, any prayer which does not give these fruits or produces opposite fruits, is a bad tree and a bad prayer, even if accompanied by raptures, ecstasies and miracles. Faith, charity and humility are the roads that lead to God; whatever causes us to walk in those paths is profitable to us, whatever makes us stray from them is hurtful. There is the sure, infallible rule, and one that can be brought home to all, for the prevention and reformation of every abuse or illusion.

I cordially salute your dear sister; tell her, please, from me that she is always to continue to allow herself to be led by the interior spirit and to remain, as she is, in complete self-abandonment in the hands of God, equally pleased with His gifts and His deprivations, and with the apparent nothingness in which He leaves her when He pleases. There lies all the perfection and the true progress of a faithful soul. Ah! How pleased God is to speak unceasingly to His spouses of that holy self-abandonment which can alone unite them solidly to Him.

Jean-Pierre de Caussade
to Mother Louise-Françoise de Rosen

9. Self-Abandonment in the Midst of Ordeals

Nancy, 1734

Dear Sister,

Thank you for the delightful letter of which you have been so happily inspired to send me a copy. I have re-read and I shall re-read it frequently with great edification. In your case I am having an experience that I have rarely had before: after having read and re-read your letter, beseeching God's help the while, I was unable to recall either what you had said to me or my answer to you. Three thoughts relating to this have occurred to me.

1. When God desires to withdraw all perceptible help from a soul, He does not allow that soul to discover any, even in its director, except in a most fleeting manner. He then constrains the soul to sustain itself by this simple thought: My state is good, since it has been deemed so by the guide it has pleased God to give me.

2. That it is scarcely necessary for God to give me a message for you, after the letter which I have deemed before God wholly to meet your need and fully to support you.

3. For all your darkness, insensibility and stupidity, your faith does not lack an unshakeable though imperceptible support, since, on the pattern of Jesus Christ, your strong desire is to abandon yourself to Him by whom you imagine yourself abandoned and left forlorn. It is a plain indication that in the midst of your apparent forlornness and your conscious self-abandonment, pure faith enables you to know and be interiorly convinced that in

truth you are anything but abandoned, anything but forlorn. The interior grief caused by fear of your inability at
such times to abandon yourself in all things, or after the
fashion which you desire, surely shows the profound and
hidden desire which you bear in the depths of your heart
for that utter self-abandonment and that meritorious
self-effacement. Does God not see such desires? and do not
all desires, deeply hidden though they be, speak more
eloquently to God than all your words? Most certainly,
such desires are acts – the best of all acts. For if you were
allowed to practise self-abandonment consciously you
would find consolation once more. Yet you would lose, at
least in part, the salutary perception of your wretchedness,
while you would be exposed anew to the unremarked
return of self-love and its disastrous complacency. You are
in far greater safety at the bottom of the abyss of pure
faith. Live there in peace, and await the Lord. Such
peaceable and humble expectancy must keep you in a state
of recollection, be counted to you for prayer, and provide
you with gentle occupation during your pious exercises.

Jean-Pierre de Caussade
to Sister Bourcier de Monthureux

3

Self-Acceptance

1. Self-Acceptance

Out of evil, much good has come to me. By keeping quiet, repressing nothing, remaining attentive, and accepting reality – taking things as they are, and not as I wanted them to be – by doing all this, unusual knowledge has come to me, and unusual powers, such as I could never have imagined before. I always thought that when we accepted things they overpowered us in some way or other. This turns out not to be true at all, and it is only by accepting them that one can assume an attitude towards them. So now I intend to play the game of life, being receptive to whatever comes to me, good or bad, sun and shadow that are forever alternating, and also in this accepting my own nature with its positive and negative sides. Thus everything becomes more alive to me. What a fool I was! How I tried to force everything to go the way I thought it ought to.

From a Former Patient
to C.G. Jung

2. Simplicity

A perfect childlike simplicity puts us at once into intimate relationship with God, without any hindrance.

*

Let us try more and more to maintain in the depths of our souls the childlike simplicity and artlessness which our Lord asks and commands. If we cannot always behave in this way in the world, it is because intelligence and goodwill are often lacking in the world. It is never because of God, to whom we are never so pleasing as when we are really like little children before Him.

*

Simplicity is the final word as regards the true way of living. It is the lesson our Lord teaches us when He declares that the Kingdom of Heaven is for children and those who are childlike. Yet as with all childlike virtues, simplicity is easily practised in childhood, but still more easily lost afterwards. It is only by a long and roundabout route that we find it again, making it triumphantly and finally ours because we have won it for ourselves.

*

The concentration which we bring to bear on our interior conduct is like that which we bring to the learning of a new language. In your case it is now time for this intensity to cease and give place to interior simplicity, leaving the soul with great freedom of movement; in the same way that after we have spoken a foreign language for some time, we leave our words to look after themselves.

Is there not a stage when we are very careful about the details of grammar, and a later stage when we need think of nothing but of speaking freely and easily? It is the same with the growth of the spirit. After having studied ourselves deeply, we must then forget all about it, go straight ahead and do our best, trusting only to that simple instinct of straightforward wisdom which is the natural side, the truth of the Christian life. What perfection of good we reach in this way without realizing it. Just as, after our grammar lessons, we acquire a surprising fluency without thinking about it as soon as we aim at nothing but speaking naturally.

*

All those souls who seek God with great depth of desire are more or less entangled in their own aspirations. God is indeed pleased with them for having carried their goodwill and their love of virtue so far; but there comes a time when peace is found rather in humble, reasonable, confident simplicity. It is then that God allows the soul whose sufferings He has accepted, to feel His *consolation* – I do not say His *consolations*. We know instinctively that God is good and we never lose sight of that fact.

*

And so you in your turn must love our Lord with simplicity; that is to say, with the entire conviction of your great unending insufficiency, yet nevertheless, content to love Him thus. Do not attempt to compete with our Lord's love; you would necessarily be defeated in such an effort. Just go on with simplicity and humility as well as you can. That will be perfection . . .

Abbé de Tourville

3. *Troubled by Sins*

9 August 1953

Christ is in our midst.

I fully sympathize with your experiences. Even now you are troubled by sins committed in your youth. The enemy of mankind, the devil, made you afraid to open your distressed heart to me when you were here at the monastery.

It is always like that; when a person commits a sin, he thinks he gets consolation from it, but after he has tasted sin, the result is the opposite: great sorrow and languor of spirit, and the poor soul feels like a fish cast ashore. It is a hard situation, and a person all but despairs. At such a difficult moment it would be good to talk to an experienced person, who could, of course, undoubtedly help.

There is no sin that is beyond God's mercy, and the sins of the whole world are like a handful of sand thrown into the sea.

But you write: "Will the Lord forgive me?" You confessed and repented. The Lord forgave you and does not remember your sins. Be sure of this (Ezekiel the prophet). In your difficult time of the past your poor soul suffered and endured the cost of sin. But now be at peace and thank God for His holy mercy.

God accepts equally the Jesus Prayer and remembrance of God. Remembrance of God suits your way of life better. Prayer of the mind must proceed under the guidance of an experienced person who himself knows about it from his experience.

The Lord keep you. I ask your holy prayers.

Staretz John

4. *You Together are Christ's Body*

Just as a human body, though it is made up of many parts, is a single unit because all these parts, though many, make one body, so it is with Christ. In the one Spirit we were all baptized, Jews as well as Greeks, slaves as well as citizens, and one Spirit was given to us all to drink.

Nor is the body to be identified with any one of its many parts. If the foot were to say, "I am not a hand and so I do not belong to the body", would that mean that it stopped being part of the body? If the ear were to say, "I am not an eye, and so I do not belong to the body", would that mean that it was not a part of the body? If your whole body was just one eye, how would you hear anything? If it was just one ear, how would you smell anything?

Instead of that, God put all the separate parts into the body on purpose. If all the parts were the same, how could it be a body? As it is, the parts are many but the body is one. The eye cannot say to the hand, "I do not need you", nor can the head say to the feet, "I do not need you."

What is more, it is precisely the parts of the body that seem to be the weakest which are the indispensable ones; and it is the least honourable parts of the body that we clothe with the greatest care. So our more improper parts get decorated in a way that our more proper parts do not need. God has arranged the body so that more dignity is given to the parts which are without it, and so that there may not be disagreements inside the body, but that each part may be equally concerned for all the others. If one part is hurt, all parts are hurt with it. If one part is given special honour, all parts enjoy it.

Now you together are Christ's body; but each of you is a different part of it. In the Church, God has given the first place to apostles, the second to prophets, the third to teachers; after them, miracles, and after them the gift of healing; helpers, good leaders, those with many languages. Are all of them apostles, or all of them prophets, or all of them teachers? Do they all have the gift of miracles, or all have the gift of healing? Do all speak strange languages, and all interpret them?

St Paul
to the Corinthians

5. *On Being Ourselves*

St Thomas Aquinas says that the angels differ as much from one another as if they belonged to different species. This is equally true of each one of us. Each human being must consider himself as a separate world, to be governed according to its own special qualities.

*

God is working on you in order that you may no longer be a child, tossed about by every wind, a prey to external influences. He has given you your own grace, your own nature (in so far as it is good), your own distinctive character. You are therefore required to be yourself and not anyone else.

*

Live according to your own nature; inwardly without restriction; outwardly in so far as external conditions permit. I would compare you to a sailor; he has no doubts as to the port for which he is making and if he is obliged to tack, it is in order to make his port. It is not that he has changed his mind; on the contrary, he makes use of the changing winds in order that their very changeableness may bring him to his port.

*

There is infinitely less disadvantage in following the right road, even though it may sometimes lead us accidentally astray, than in keeping to a wrong road where we get confused, go round and round in circles and never reach any desirable goal in the end. Follow the route I have mapped out for you without being discouraged, even although you may sometimes meet with difficulties. That is only to be expected.

For the difficulties of a thing are part of its very nature. There is nothing in this world without its difficulties, and we must accept them with tranquillity and wisdom.

*

One of the hardest but one of the most absolutely necessary things is to follow our own particular line of development, side by side with souls who have quite a different one; often one opposed to our own. It is natural for youth to hesitate between an attitude which it fears may be presumptuous and a candid admission of inferiority to everything around it. But this hesitation must cease or we shall never grow up. We must be ourselves and not try to get inside someone else's skin. David could have done nothing in the armour of Saul; he refused it and ran to fetch his sling and some pebbles from the brook. It was with these he slew Goliath, the symbol of the devil as the Holy Fathers taught. Still less must we look for approval and appreciation as a sign that we are on the right path. There are not so many good judges as all that, and the judgement of common opinion is far from being common sense. Good judges are so rare that St Francis de Sales could declare, "It is said that only one in a thousand is a true spiritual director. I say only one in ten thousand!" We must therefore free ourselves absolutely of this anxious desire to be at one with other souls, however virtuous or wise they may be; just as we must never expect them to see things through our eyes. We must follow our own light as though we were alone in the world, save as regards charity to others. In purely private matters, we must never be deflected from our own path.

The moral and religious teaching of this century has, either through ignorance or stupidity, given us a false standard of virtue. It is a standard reached by no one, and those who think they reach it are very innocent and more to be pitied than those who lament in vain that they always fall short of it. We have forgotten St Paul's two interrelated pieces of advice (i) *Sapere ad sobrietatem*, which means, "be wise with moderation" and not to excess; never straining beyond our nature, beyond the grace we have been given, beyond our powers and our means. We are not to dream of perfection in the abstract but to try to achieve our own special kind of perfection which depends on our character and our circumstances. And St Paul's second piece of advice (ii) "God has distributed His gifts: some are prophets, some teachers, some interpreters" and so on. Each differs in grace as each member of the body differs in function.

This grand and simple teaching has now been superseded by one which is extreme and exaggerated, a distilled perfection. It is no longer simple but overstrained, made up of all that is most exceptional in exceptional characters. This standard is then set for all and we are told that there is no other; that there is only one kind of perfection and that it is therefore the same for everybody. We can realize what spiritual struggles this teaching provokes and how souls try to adopt a form of perfection which renders them as helpless as David would have been in Saul's magnificent armour.

We are the brothers and sisters of the Saints. They became holy in their way; we must become holy in ours, not in theirs. Otherwise sanctity would be for us nothing but a wearisome routine for which nevertheless we could not blame such holy souls. They lived before us and did not absolve us from the responsibility of independent thought or of deciding for ourselves as to what suits us best. Why should we always give pre-eminence to the minds of the dead rather than to those of the living? What a strange method of progress that would give to sanctity! Why, for instance, in the religious life are solitaries not still trained after the model of *St Madeleine à la Sainte-Baume* or of St Mary of Egypt in the desert? . . . Come! Come! we must wake up and try to be that which we are reasonably meant to be and not that which other people have been. One does not become holy by copying others but by making good use of what is truly part of oneself . . .

*

Every Saint is a pattern; but no Saint is a pattern of everything. The practical question for us is not to know whether they became Saints or not — we know that they did — but what Saints, in order to reach sanctity, have had to follow the path which God has made peculiarly ours.

*

Therefore leave your soul too, to pray as suits it best, in its own way, without strain. Allow it most of the time to remain quite still. Pray along the lines which show you the needs of the world and which interest you. Nothing could be better. In a word, follow your bent; your need of quiet or of doing nothing according to what seems most natural to you at the time.

*

When your soul begins to feel more at home, it will be easier to find out what is usually for you the quickest way of coming into the close and living presence of Jesus Christ. You will then be able to develop this special bent with greater certainty and will gradually discover the endless variety of ways in which it can grow. You will thus have cleared your path. For nothing is more individual to each soul than the form of its intimacy with our Lord. His earthly life, as it reveals to our eyes and ears His relationships with souls, reveals also that no two were intimate with Him in the same sort of way. Here again, observe the path you take instinctively at those times when you are most keenly aware of the real, actual and intimate presence of our Lord. Realize that there lies your own particular grace.

Abbé de Tourville

6. *Bearing with Oneself*

Dear Sister,

We have to submit ourselves to God in all things and for all things, whether it be the station and the circumstances in which He has placed us, the good and ill fortune which He has allotted us, even the character, intelligence, disposition, temperament and tendencies with which He has equipped us. Practise patience in your own affairs and perfect submission to the will of God. When you have made such patience yours, you will enjoy that great peace which nothing can disturb, into which no self-recrimination can enter, and you will put up with yourself with the same gentleness as you must show to others. This matter is more important than you think: just now there is nothing, possibly, more essential to your sanctification. Never lose sight of it, then, but constantly perform acts of submission to God's blessed will, and acts of charity, forbearance and sweetness for yourself even more than for others.

Before this is possible you will need to put great constraint upon yourself.

A soul to which God has revealed its shortcomings is far more of a burden to itself than its neighbour can be. For, however near he be, that neighbour is not always by our side, while in no case is he within us. We are our own burden, on the other hand; we cannot escape ourselves for a single moment, nor lose ourselves from sight and feeling, nor cease from trailing everywhere we go our imperfections and our failings. The supreme manifestation of God's infinite goodness lies in the fact that the sorrow and the shame these failings cause us, cure us of them, always provided that the shame does not become vexation and that the sorrow is inspired by love of God and not by self-love. Sorrow born of self-love is full of perturbation and bitterness: far from healing our soul's wounds it serves only to pour poison into them. On the contrary, sorrow springing from love of God is serene and full of abandonment. While it abhors the fault, it delights in the humiliation which is its sequel: as a consequence it gives all the credit to the humiliation, thus making loss itself an opportunity for gain.

No longer, then, torment yourself on account of your failings and of the imperfection of your works. Make God an offering of the sorrow that imperfection brings you, and allow His merciful Providence to redeem these small infidelities by small afflictions and troubles of every kind. Let patience be your one weapon; after a fall pick yourself up as speedily as possible, lamenting the tumble only with meek and tranquil humility. God wills it thus. Moreover, by such unwearied patience, you render Him more glory and yourself make more progress than you could ever do by the most violent effort.

Jean-Pierre de Caussade

7. *On Gratitude*

Forgetfulness of self, of which we often hear as pertaining to those who seek after God in a generous spirit, does not interfere with gratitude for His Gifts. And for this reason: such forgetfulness does not lie in not being conscious of anything we possess, but rather in never confining ourselves to the contemplation of self, or dwelling upon our own good or evil in an exclusive or personal fashion. All such self-occupation severs us from pure and simple love, narrows the heart, and sets us further from true perfection by dint of seeking it in an excited, anxious, restless spirit, which comes of self-love.

But though we may forget ourselves, that is to say, we may not be studying self-interest alone, we shall not fail often to see ourselves truly. We shall not contemplate self out of egotism, but as we contemplate God there will often be a side light, so to say, thrown upon ourselves; just as a man who stands looking at the reflection of another in a large mirror, while looking for that other man he beholds himself, without seeking to do so. And thus we often see ourselves clearly, in the pure light of God. The Presence of God in purity and simplicity, sought after in very faithfulness, is like that large mirror, wherein we discern the tiniest spot that flecks our soul.

A peasant who has never passed beyond his own poor village realizes its poverty but faintly. But set him amid splendid palaces and courts, and he will perceive how squalid his own home is, and how vile his rags compared with such magnificence. Even so we realize our own loathsomeness and unworthiness when brought face to face with the beauty and greatness of God.

Talk as much as you will of the vanity and emptiness of the creature, the shortness and uncertainty of life, the inconstancy of fortune and friends, the delusions of grandeur, its inevitable and bitter disappointments, the failure of bright hopes, the void of all we attain, and the poignancy of the evils we endure; all those things, true and just as they are, do not touch the heart, they do not reach far, or alter a man's life. He sighs over the bondage of vanity, yet does not seek to break his bonds. But let one ray of heavenly light penetrate within, and forthwith beholding the depth of goodness, which is God, he likewise beholds the depth of evil, His fallen creature. Then he despises himself, hates, shuns, fears, renounces self; he throws himself upon God and is lost in Him. Thus it is that "one deep telleth another". Verily that man's loss is a blessed one, for he finds himself without seeking. He has no more selfish interests, but all turns to his profit, for everything turns to good for those who love God. He sees the mercies which issue forth from that abyss of weakness, sin, and nothingness; he sees and rejoices. And here observe that those who have not as yet made any great progress in self-renunciation still see all these mercies very much from the side which bears personal reference to themselves. For thorough setting aside of self-will is so rare in this life, that very few souls are able to look at the mercies they have received from anything but their own point of view; they rejoice in the All-powerful Hand which has saved them, so to say, in spite of themselves. But a really pure, wholly self-detached soul, such as are the Saints in Heaven, would feel the same joy and love over the mercies poured forth on others as on themselves; for, wholly forgetting self, they would love the Good Pleasure of God, the riches of His Grace, and His Glory, as set forth in the sanctification of others, as much as in their own. All would be the same, because "I" ceased to be: it would be no more "I" than another, but God Alone in all, to be loved, adored, and the sole joy of true, disinterested love. Such a soul is rapt in wonder at His Mercies, not for its own sake, but for love of Him. It thanks Him that He has done His Will and glorified Himself, even as in the Lord's Prayer we ask Him that it may be done, and that His Kingdom may come. . . . But short of this blessed state, the soul is touched with gratitude for the benefits of which it is conscious; and as nothing is more dangerous than any attempt to soar beyond our vocation, so nothing is more harmful to the spiritual life than to lose sight of such sustenance as is suitable to its actual needs, by aiming at a higher standard of perfection than is fitted to us. When the soul feels deeply moved with gratitude for all God has done for it, such gratitude should be cherished carefully, waiting till the time when God may see fit to purify it still more from all elements of self. The child who attempts to walk alone before its time is sure to fall; he must not tear off the leading-strings with which his nurse upholds him. Let us be content to live on gratitude, and be sure that though there may be a mingling of self-interest in it, it will strengthen our heart. Let us love God's Mercies, not merely for Himself and His Glory, but for ourselves and our eternal happiness; if eventually God should enlarge our hearts to contain a purer, more generous love, a love more unreservedly His, then we may safely and unhesitatingly yield to that more perfect love.

While, then, you adore God's Mercy, and are filled with wondering admiration at it; while you long above all things to fulfil His Will; while you marvel at the goodness with which He has made what seemed a "vessel of dishonour" to be unto honour, pour out the most abundant thanksgiving of which you are capable; and remember that the purest of all God's Gifts is the power of loving them all for His Sake, not for your own.

François Fénelon

8. *Humility*

Let us content ourselves with being as little evil as we can. That done, all is well.

*

Perfection never exists apart from imperfection, just as good health cannot exist without our feeling effort, fatigue, heat or cold, hunger or thirst; yet none of those prevent the enjoyment of good health.

*

If you attempt to do all that is possible, all that is desirable, all that might be edifying, you will never succeed. Such an aim would indeed lack simplicity, humility, and frankness; and those three qualities are worth more than everything else to which you might aspire, however good your motives.

*

Perfection consists not in taking the safest course (sometimes quite the opposite) but in doing the least possible evil, having regard to our state of mind at the time and to the difficulties of our nature. It consists also in modestly holding fast to a very great simplicity, renouncing any course of action which although it either is, or appears to be, more perfect in itself, would strain our powers.

I wish so much that you could get hold of the idea of what perfection in this world consists of. It is not like going up a great hill from which we see an ever-widening landscape, a greater horizon, a plain receding further and further into the distance. It is more like an overgrown path which we cannot find; we grope about; we are caught by brambles; we lose all sense of the distance covered; we do not know whether we are going round and round or whether we are advancing. We are certain only of one thing; that we desire to go on even though we are worn and tired. That is your life and you should rejoice greatly because of it, for it is a true life, serious and real, on which God opens His eyes and His heart.

*

We are far too apt to think of virtue as a broad, smooth road, whereas it is really a very rough and narrow one. It never becomes smooth or less uneven, until we observe that, in spite of all the jolting, we do manage to stay on it and even to advance a little, thanks to our Lord who holds us. Our confidence in Him, gained by experience, gives us a certain inward tranquillity in spite of the jolting. That is what is meant by the smooth road.

*

Our Lord does not plan interior splendours or exterior results for us in this world, but rather desolation, both within and without, to be endured as well as we can; that is the ideal. You must admit that from the moral point of view, this ideal is sublime and that it is admirably suited to human nature and to our earthly life. You will also observe that it is realized every day, which cannot be said of any other ideal.

*

It has been said that there are on the battlefield, defeats as glorious as victories. That is true also of the daily defeats of the soul in the struggle which we begin afresh every day, making new plans to do better and experimenting with new ideas and methods in order to succeed. That is what the Gospel declares: "Happy is the servant whom when his Master cometh He shall find . . ." Find how? Victorious? Triumphant? His task fully accomplished? No! Rather he who shall be found watching, vigilant, wide awake; that is to say looking after the things which are not going well and putting them right, time after time. That is our really great merit in the sight of God. Do not be surprised because I say *great*, even though in itself the merit is very small. It is great, because we are extremely weak and because God knows, as the Bible says, the clay of which we are made. God has ordered this world so that little things may become great, fitted as they are to our puny stature.

*

Let us put up with ourselves in charity and try to rule ourselves as we should like to rule others. That is to say, using towards ourselves much gentle and persuasive skill, which will turn us inside out as delicately as we turn a glove.

*

Use all your intelligence and experience in managing your own life, employing the tenderness you would expect to find in a being of ideal kindness. What I am asking you, in the name of our Lord, is to have charity towards yourself.

*

I know only too well the effect any disorder in the physical machinery has on the soul. Only the fatherly goodness of God knows how to compensate for this by attributing immense value to the sufferings and conflicts of the soul which labours under physical disabilities, and by assessing at zero almost all the failings and misdeeds which result more or less directly from bodily suffering.

Praise God! for I assure you that He is more compassionate than words can express. Be filled then with rejoicing; not because of your ills which are in themselves bad and must be cured, but because of the tenderness of God, who, with His fatherly and loving heart understands all your difficulties. Keep your inward peace therefore, however disturbed and distracted you may feel. Try to be as indulgent towards the poverty and faultiness of your soul as God Himself is.

*

To remain in a certain state of soul is to progress, just as agricultural progress on the land consists in doing the same work on the farm every day, ploughing the same number of furrows in the same way.

What I should like, therefore, in your case, is a feeling of rest. Say to yourself, "I please God just as I am at this moment", and that even while taking your moral wretchedness into account. For there is no state of soul in which God does not make great allowances for our infirmities, thus showing His indulgence and His mercy. We must accept this, not proudly, but with loving gratitude and a growing sense of the loving-kindness of our Lord.

Moreover what I am asking of you in the name of your Saviour, is not stagnation, and you will realize this increasingly. For as you come more and more to accept the state of your soul as satisfactory, you will find greater freedom of spirit, greater joy and greater peace of soul. And all this will immensely strengthen you.

Abbé de Tourville

9. *The Tendency to Condemn Ourselves*

4 January 1952

. . . You keep condemning yourself and regarding yourself as good for nothing and the worst of all people, but these are only words with you. You feel that you are not bad. If you felt the way you say you do, you would not condemn others for anything and you would not feel insulted over my having called N more intelligent than you. Ha-ha-ha! How muddle-headed you are. You go on to write that I should pray and beg the Lord to "make you good". Again what a muddle-headed request! Another laugh: she will live in an off-hand way and the old man will beg and pray God that she should become good. But this is not in accord with spiritual knowledge; neither God nor I can help you if you yourself do not work at it devotedly, the Holy Fathers have said.

Yesterday a monk came to me and said: "I have a very big sin and I do not know whether the Lord will forgive me." I asked: "What is it?" "Blasphemy against God and the Holy Mysteries." I said to him: "In these thoughts there is no sin, for they are from the devil and are called suggestions; they are not sins. Do not pay attention to them and lift your mind to some scriptural subject." I talked further with him on this subject and gave him John of the Ladder to read about blasphemous thoughts [23, 38ff.].

Today, 4 January, the Holy Church celebrates the seventy Holy Apostles. Of these, five Apostles fell away: Judas, Nicholas (he was a bishop), Phygelus (he was a bishop), Hermogenes (he too was a bishop), and Demas (he was a priest and became a worshipper of idols). I used to wonder: Why did the Lord choose them as Apostles to preach? He knew that they would fall away. But once during a service it somehow became clear to me that the Lord in His mercy calls everyone to Himself, but He does not destroy our free will. And if someone willingly turns from virtue to a depraved life – he is himself to blame, since he did not make the effort with his free will to please God. One became fond of money, another became fond of this temporal life, and the others the same. We should use our free will to work to please God; then grace helps us. But if we do not make the effort, even God's grace will not help; our work and God's grace go together.

Staretz John

10. Fearfulness

Do not be afraid; you insult God by mistrusting His goodness; He knows better than you what you want and are able to bear; He will never try you beyond your strength. So I repeat it; fear nothing, O you of little faith! The experience of your own weakness shows you how little you can reckon on yourself or your best resolutions. Sometimes one might suppose, to see the warmth of one's feelings, that nothing could throw one back, and then, after having exclaimed, like St Peter, "Though I should die with Thee, yet will I not deny Thee!" one ends like him by being frightened at a servant maid, and denying our Lord! Weak indeed we are! but while such weakness is deplorable, the realization thereof is most useful if it strips us of all self-reliance. A weakness which we know and which humbles us is worth more than the most angelic goodness complacently self-appropriated! So be weak and depressed if God permits it; but at all events be humble, frank, and docile in your depression. Some day you will laugh at all your present fears, and will thank God for all that I say so harshly to drive you out of your timid prudence.

François Fénelon

4

Prayer and Contemplation

1. The Desert

I am going to lure them away,
lead them into the desert
and speak to their hearts.

God is bestowing a special favour on you by drawing you into the desert. The call is a matter of God's free choice; you will only be able to persevere in it by His condescension. You will always remember how privileged you are that God should love your soul, and as time goes by you will appreciate this all the more. At the outset, in spite of what you have read and what you call your experience, you will not know what the loneliness of the desert has in store for you.

There, as elsewhere, no two souls follow precisely the same path, and God never repeats Himself in His creatures. Very rarely, if at all, does He reveal His designs in advance.

Humble and detached, go into the desert. For God, awaiting you there, you bring nothing worth having, except your entire availability. The lighter your baggage is, the poorer you will be in what the world esteems, and the greater will be your chances of success, since God will be all the freer to use you. He is calling you to live on friendly terms with Him: to nothing else.

To influence others directly, even by the pen, is not one of the pursuits envisaged for the desert. You must be content to lose yourself entirely. If you secretly desire to be or to become "somebody", you are doomed to failure. The desert is pitiless; it infallibly rejects all self-seekers.

Let us go in, in holy nakedness . . .

A Cistercian
to a Novice

2. On Offering One's Whole Being to God

Well, then, all I ask you to do is to think – without any subtle investigations – that you are as you are, no matter how foul or wretched you may be – as long as you have been forgiven (as I take for granted) all your particular and general sins in the right way – in accordance, that is, with the true teaching of the Church. (If that isn't the case, then neither you nor anyone else may dare to start this exercise, or may not start it with my agreement.) If you really feel that you have done everything you can in that regard, then you can start the exercise. Even if you still think that you are quite vile and disgusting, and that your own self is such a nuisance, and that it cramps you so that you hardly know what is the best thing to do with yourself, you must still do what I tell you exactly as I tell you.

What you must do is to take the good gracious God, just as He is, without any qualification, and to attach Him like a poultice to your sick self, just as you are. Or, if you like, raise up your sick self, just as you are, and try by desire to touch the good gracious God just as He is. Touching God is everlasting health, as we know from the woman in the Gospel: "All I have to do to be safe is to touch the hem of His clothes." The supreme heavenly touch of God's own being, of His own dear self, will do much more to get rid of your sickness, so go right ahead and use this miraculous medicine. Raise up your sick self, just as you are, to the gracious God, just as He is, without speculating and without special investigation of any characteristic of your own being or of God's, whether healthy or unhealthy, given by grace or by nature, divine or human. All you have to do now is to ensure that your hidden contemplation of the very essence of your being is raised up in gladness and loving desire, to be united and made one in grace and spirit with the precious being of God just as He is in Himself, and no more than that.

If your wayward and inquisitive reason can't get anything out of this exercise and starts nagging you continually, prompting you to give it all up and do something really concrete and worthwhile in its subtle investigative way (it thinks what you're doing is useless merely because it knows nothing of or about it), I find that a good sign – all the better: it means that what you're doing is much more valuable than anything it can do. I find it all the better because there is nothing that I could do, and nothing that my investigative reason could manage, within or without, that could get me so close to God and so far from the world, as this simple, almost invisible experience of offering up the very essence of my being.

Even though your rational mind can't find anything worthwhile or healthy in this exercise, and therefore would like to stop you doing it, don't on any account – and certainly not because your reason is critical – stop trying. Be the boss as far as it's concerned. Don't stop short in your tracks, let alone go back to the beginning, however much fuss and noise your rational objections make. You nourish your rational mind when you allow it to speculate and investigate the various characteristics of your being. That kind of meditation can be valuable, even profitable, in its own right, but, if set against the hidden contemplation and offering up of your being that I have recommended, it will only split and divide the perfect unity which ought to persist between God and your soul. So don't stop. Carry on with the exercise at the lowest rung of your spirit or being. Don't turn round and go back for any reason, no matter how good or holy the thing that your rational mind asks you to pursue may seem to be.

The Author of
The Cloud of Unknowing

3. On Silence and Recollection

I think that you should try hard to learn to practise silence, so far as general courtesy will admit of. Silence promotes the Presence of God, avoids many harsh or proud words, suppresses many dangers in the way of ridiculing or rashly judging our neighbours. Silence humbles the mind, and detaches it from the world; it would create a kind of solitude in the heart like that you need under present difficulties. If you retrenched all useless talk, you would have many available moments even amid the inevitable claims of society. You wish for freedom for prayer; while God, who knows what you need better than you do, surrounds you with restraints and hampering claims. The hindrances which beset you in the order of God's Providence will profit you more than any possible self-delectation in devotion. You know very well that retirement is not essential to the love of God. When He gives you time, you must take it and use it; but meanwhile abide patiently, satisfied that whatever He allots you is best. Lift up your heart to Him continually, without making any outward sign; only talk when it is necessary, and bear quietly with what crosses you. As you grow in the faith, God will treat you accordingly. You stand more in need of mortification than of light. The only thing I dread for you is dissipation; but you may remedy even that by silence. If you are steadfast in keeping silence when it is not necessary to speak, God will preserve you from evil when it is right for you to talk.

If you are unable to secure much time to yourself, be all the more careful about stray moments. Even a few minutes gleaned faithfully amid engagements will be more profitable in God's sight than whole hours given up to Him at freer seasons. Moreover, many brief spaces of time through the day will amount to something considerable at last. Possibly you yourself may find the advantage of such frequent recollection in God's Presence more than in a regular definite period allotted to devotion.

Your lot is to love, to be silent, and to sacrifice your inclinations, in order to fulfil the Will of God by moulding yourself to that of others. Happy indeed you are thus to bear a cross laid on you by God's own hands in the order of His Providence. The penitential work we choose, or even accept at the hands of others, does not so stifle self-love as that which God assigns us from day to day. In it we find nothing to foster self, and, coming as it does directly from His Merciful Providence, it brings with it grace sufficient for all our needs. All we have to do is to give ourselves up to God day by day, without looking further; He will carry us in His Arms as a loving mother carries her child. Let us believe, hope, love, with a child's simplicity, in every need looking with affection and trust to our Heavenly Father. He has said in His own word, "Can a Woman forget her sucking child? . . . Yea, she may forget, yet will I not forget thee."

François Fénelon

4. On Prayer

A.D. 411

You asked me, I remember, to write you something on prayer, and I promised to do so as soon as He to whom we pray should give me time and opportunity. So I now feel it my bounden duty to discharge my debt and in the love of

Christ meet your devout request. How much your desire gladdened me as showing your high sense of a high duty, words cannot express.

In the darkness of this world where pilgrim-wise we journey far from the Lord, as long as we walk by faith and not by sight (2 Corinthians 5:6–7), the Christian soul ought to account itself desolate and never cease to pray, learning to fix the eye of faith on the divine word of the holy Scriptures as *on a light shining in a dark place until the day dawn and the day-star arise in our hearts* (2 Peter 1:19). For the ineffable source from which this lamp borrows its light is the Light that shines in darkness but the darkness does not comprehend it. To see it, our hearts must be purified by faith: *Blessed are the clean of heart for they shall see God* (Matthew 5:8); and *We know that when He shall appear we shall be like to Him, because we shall see Him as He is* (1 John 3:2) – after death, true life; after desolation, true consolation; a life which delivers our souls from death and a consolation which restrains our eyes from tears.

Why do we scatter our desires and why fear that we shall not pray as we ought and why ask therefore what to pray for? Why not rather say with the Psalmist: *One thing I have asked of the Lord, this will I seek after; that I may dwell in the house of the Lord all the days of my life; that I may see the delight of the Lord and may visit His temple.* For there *all the days* are not differentiated by their coming and going: the beginning of one is not the end of another: they are all unending, constituting as they do a life which is itself without end. In order to obtain this life of bliss, true blissful Life Himself has taught us to pray, not in long rigmaroles as though the more wordy we were, the surer we were heard, because we are addressing One who, as our Lord tells us, knows what is needful for us before we ask Him (Matthew 6:7, 8). It may seem surprising, however, that after forbidding us to speak much, He who knows what we need before we ask should say to us: *Men ought always to pray and faint not.* He proceeds to give us the example of the widow who desired revenge against an enemy. By her constant entreaties she forced an unjust judge to give way not from motives of justice or mercy, but overcome through sheer weariness of her importunity. So we are taught how our merciful and just Lord God will of a certainty give ear to persevering prayer, when this widow by dint of continual begging prevailed over the indifference of an unjust and wicked judge. Moreover, she obtained her desire which was nothing less than vengeance, and so what will be the readiness and loving-kindness with which God will fulfil the holy desires of those who He knows have forgiven others their trespasses? Our Lord gives us a similar lesson in the story of the man visited by a friend on a journey. The man had not the wherewithal to set a meal before him and wanted to borrow three loaves from another friend of his – in which, perhaps, there is a figure of the Trinity of Persons in one substance. Finding him and all his servants asleep he knocked in a way so persistent and so annoying that the friend was completely roused from his slumbers and gave him as many as he wanted, not because he felt at all kindly disposed towards him but simply to avoid further disturbance. Therefore if a man is forced to give away even against his will because someone in need would give him no rest until he did, with how much more merciful kindness will He give who never sleeps but rather rouses us from sleep to make us ask from Him?

It is to impress this lesson upon us that He adds: *Ask, and it shall be given you; seek and you shall find; knock, and it shall be opened to you. For everyone that asketh receiveth; and he that seeketh findeth; and to him that knocketh it shall be opened. And which of you, if he ask his father bread, will he give him a stone? Or a fish, will he for a fish give him a serpent? Or if he shall ask an egg, will he reach him a scorpion? If you then, being evil, know how to give good gifts to your children, how much more will your Father from heaven give the good Spirit to them that ask him?* (Luke 11: 9–13). We have here those three things commended by the Apostle: by the fish is signified faith, either because of the water of Baptism, or because it remains unharmed amid the tempestuous waves of this world; in contrast with which is the serpent that with his poisonous guile persuaded men to disbelieve God. By the egg is signified hope, because the life of the young bird is not yet evident but is to be – it is not seen but hoped for, because *hope which is seen is not hope* (Romans 8:24); in contrast with which is the scorpion, for the man who hopes for eternal life forgets the things that are behind and stretches forth to those that lie before, since it is dangerous to look back; but the scorpion is to be feared because of what lies in its tail – its sharp and poisonous sting. Bread signifies charity, for *the greatest of these is charity* (1 Corinthians 13:13) and bread surpasses all other food in worth; in contrast to which is the stone, for hearts that are hardened refuse to exercise charity.

Thus when we practise faith, hope and charity with continual desire, we pray always. But at the same time we also set aside stated hours and times devoted to explicit prayer to God according to the Apostle's instruction: *Let your petitions be made known to God* (Philippians 4: 6), not indeed as though we are giving God information, because He knows them before we say a word, but rather that in the presence of God we ourselves should realize all we need and wait patiently upon Him. It is, therefore, neither wrong nor unprofitable to spend a long time in prayer (although, as I have said, in desire we ought always to be in an attitude of prayer), provided that we do not neglect other good and necessary works. To spend a long time in prayer is not, as some think, the same as praying "with much speaking". Multiplied words are one thing, long-continued warmth of desire is another. It is written of our Lord Himself that He spent the whole night in prayer and that being in an agony He prayed the longer.

We are told how the monks of Egypt prayed very frequently but very briefly. Their prayer was sudden and ejaculatory so that the intense application so necessary in prayer should not vanish or lose its keenness by a slow performance. By this practice they show clearly enough that just as, on the one hand, this close attention must not be exhausted if it cannot last long, on the other hand, if it can be sustained it must not be abruptly snapped. Far be it from us to spend our prayer in much speaking, or to refuse to pray much so long as the soul is rapt in fervent intensity. To speak much is to employ a superfluity of words to ask for the one thing necessary, but to pray much is to have a heart throbbing with a glowing abiding love for Him to whom we pray. Usually prayer is a question of groaning rather than speaking, tears rather than words. For He sets our tears in His sight and our groaning is not hidden from Him who made all things by His Word and does not ask for words of man.

For us human beings, however, words are a necessity, not because they acquaint God with what we want or change His designs but because they help us to see into ourselves and face our needs. When therefore we say: *Hallowed be thy name*, we stir up in ourselves the desire that God's name, essentially holy in itself, may also be esteemed holy by men and not despised; it brings no profit to God but to men. And when we say: *Thy kingdom come*, although it is bound to come whether we wish it or not, we arouse a longing in our own souls for that kingdom, that it may come within ourselves, that we may be found worthy to reign therein. When we say: *Thy will be done on earth as it is in heaven*, we beg of God the grace of obedience so that we may do His will as the angels do in the heavens. When we say: *Give us this day our daily bread*, we use the word "today" to signify this present life and ask for a sufficiency of temporal blessings; and because bread exceeds all the rest in value it is used to express the whole of our needs: or else we refer to the Sacrament of faith which we are bound to receive in this present life, not indeed for this present life but to obtain the happiness of eternal life. When we say: *Forgive us our trespasses as we forgive them that trespass against us*, we remind ourselves that what we are asking for, the same have we to do; we must merit the boon of forgiveness. When we say: *Lead us not into temptation*, we call to mind how we are to beg God not to withdraw His help for fear we be deceived and in our weakness yield to some temptation or be overcome by its strength. When we say: *Deliver us from evil*, we reflect upon the fact that we are not yet in possession of that bliss where no ill is to be suffered. And this last petition of the Lord's prayer is so comprehensive that in whatever trouble he finds himself, a Christian may well use it to give utterance to his tears and vent his groans, he may begin his prayer with this petition, employ it throughout and conclude with it.

For whatever other words we use, if we pray rightly and fittingly, we say nothing more than is already to be found in the Lord's prayer. Whosoever asks for anything that cannot find its place in that prayer from the Gospel is making, if not exactly unlawful, at least unspiritual prayer. If you run through the petitions of all holy prayers, I believe that you will find nothing that is not summed up and contained in the Lord's prayer. In praying, therefore, we are quite free to use any words that please us, but we must ask for the same things. We are left no choice in the matter. It is faith, hope and charity that lead to God the soul that prays, i.e. the soul that believes, hopes, desires and seeks for guidance as to what to ask God by a study of the Lord's prayer. And whoever begs from God that "one thing" and seeks after it, does so in perfect confidence, because that one thing is the only true, the only happy life in which, with bodies and souls immortal and incorruptible, we shall contemplate the joy of the Lord for evermore. All other things we desire and quite rightly demand with a view to this one end. In it is the fountain of life for which we now thirst in prayer as long as we live in hope, not yet seeing the things we hope for, trusting under the covert of His wings before whom is all our desire, that we may be inebriated with the plenty of His house and made to drink of the torrent of His pleasure. For with Him is the fountain of life and in His light we shall see light (Psalm 35:8–10).

St Augustine
to a Noble Lady

5. An Oratory of the Heart

He lays not great burden upon us: a little remembrance of Him from time to time; a little adoration; sometimes to pray for His grace, sometimes to offer Him your sorrows, and sometimes to return Him thanks for the benefits He has given you, and still gives you, in the midst of your troubles.

He asks you to console yourself with Him the oftenest you can. Lift up your heart to Him even at your meals and when you are in company; the least little remembrance will always be acceptable to Him.

To be with God, there is no need to be continually in church. We may make an oratory of the heart wherein to retire from time to time to converse with Him in humility, meekness and love.

Everyone is capable of familiar conversation with God, some more, some less. He knows what we can do. Let us begin then. Perhaps He is just waiting for one generous resolution on our part.

Have courage. We have but little time to live; you are near

sixty-four, and I am almost eighty. Let us live and die with God. Sufferings will be sweet and pleasant to us while we are with Him; and without Him, the greatest pleasures will be anguish to us. May He be blessed for all. Amen.

Brother Lawrence

6. *Meditation on Jesus Christ*

Do you think that you would ever be able to do this exercise without using your ordinary reason? Not at all. Not even by such acceptable meditations, carefully planned, clever and ingenious, as you are used to. Not even if they are about your sinfulness, Christ's passion, the joys of our Lady or those of all the saints and angels in heaven, or any quality or subtlety or condition that has to do with your own being or that of God. As for myself, I would prefer that naked, blind self-consciousness which I have already touched on (consciousness, that is, not of my behaviour, but of myself).

There are a lot of people who identify themselves with what they do, but that is wrong. I myself, the doer, is one thing, and what I do is another. It is the same with God. He Himself is one thing; what He does is another. Rather than take pleasure in all the ingenious, clever and well-thought-out meditations anyone can devise or mug up in books, however holy and valuable they seem to your sharp and subtle speculation, I would prefer to break my heart in weeping because I am not conscious of God in this way, and feel the anguish and weight of my own self, and thus increase my loving desire to have and to long for divine awareness.

All the same, those meditations are valuable. They are the best way for a sinner to take when he is converted to spiritual consciousness of his own self and of God. I would go so far as to say that the human mind can't think that it's possible (remembering that for God all things are possible), for a sinner eventually to be spiritually conscious of himself and of God, unless first of all he or she sees and experiences with the mind's eye and through meditation his or her own earthly behaviour and God's action on earth, and is sorry for what deserves sorrow and rejoices at what requires rejoicing. Anyone who doesn't take this way in to God, doesn't enter in all, and therefore has to stand outside, and remains standing there even when he or she thinks, well at least I'm safe inside! There are an awful lot of people who think that they're inside that spiritual door when in fact they're outside, and will stay there until they look for the door humbly. Some people find the door almost before they've looked for it, and come in before others – but that is obviously the doorkeeper's doing and nothing to do with any payment by them or with what they deserve.

The spiritual life is a marvellous household. Our Lord Himself is not only the doorkeeper but the door itself. He is the doorkeeper by His Godhead and the door by His manhood. That is what He Himself says in the gospel: "I am the door. If anyone enters by me he will be saved, and will go in and out and find pasture. The thief comes only to steal and kill and destroy." You can take this in our context as meaning the following: "I who am almighty by My Godhead may, as the doorkeeper, let in whom I want and in any way I want. But because I want there to be a common plain way for everyone, and one open entry for anyone who comes along seeking entry, so that no one can say that he or she doesn't know the way, I have clothed Myself in the common nature of mankind, and made Myself so open that I am the door by reason of My manhood. Whoever enters through Me will be safe."

They enter by the door who contemplate Christ's passion and are sorry for their wicked acts which caused that passion, bitterly reproving themselves for deserving to suffer yet not suffering, and feeling pity and compassion for their worthy Lord who suffered so vilely and yet didn't deserve to at all. Then they lift up their hearts to contemplate the love and goodness of His Godhead, in which He decided to make Himself so low and humble as to enter our mortal humanity. All those people will enter by the door and find safety. Whether they go right in and behold the love and goodness of His Godhead, or remain outside and behold the suffering of His manhood, they will have enough spiritual food for their devotion – more than enough to make their souls safe and healthy, even though they never get any further in this life.

But anyone, whoever he or she is, who doesn't go in by this door but tries to get to a perfect state by some other means, even by crazy mental speculation, avoiding the plain, common way I have described and the good advice of our spiritual fathers, is not only a night thief but a day skulker. Such people are night thieves because they go about in the darkness of sin, presuming that the strength of their own intellects and force of will could see them through, rather than trusting in good advice or the plain ordinary way I have told you of. They are day skulkers because, disguised as practitioners of the contemplative life, they steal the outward signs and words proper to contemplation without having its fruits. Because now and again they feel in themselves, in their clever minds, something like a desire to get close to God and are quite overcome by this experience, they think that everything they do is good, when actually nothing is more dangerous than for a young person to follow his or her own fierce desires without good advice and guidance. This is particularly important if their desire is set on ascending to higher things which are not only higher than they are but raised up above the plain ordinary way of Christians, as I have described it. That way, as Christ teaches, may be called the door of devotion, and the most secure entry to contemplation to be met with in this life.

The Author of
The Cloud of Unknowing

7. *God and the Human Soul*

From now on a kind of intimacy begins to grow between God and a human soul; there is also a certain kindling of love, inasmuch as the soul often feels not only that it has been visited by God and consoled by His coming, but often as if it has been filled with an unspeakable joy. Leah first felt this intimacy and kindling of love when, after the birth of Levi, she cried out mightily: "Now my husband will be joined to me!" The true spouse of our soul is God, and we are truly joined to Him when we draw close to Him in hope and true love. Just as hope is followed by love, so Judah, Leah's fourth son, was born after Levi. When he was born Leah cried out: "Now I shall praise the Lord." Hence Judah is called "praise" in the story. A human soul in love to this degree openly offers it to God, and says: "Now I shall praise the Lord." Before a soul feels this love, all that it does is done far more out of fear than out of love, but in this state a soul feels that God is so sweet, merciful, good, courteous, true, kind, faithful, loving and intimate, that there is nothing left that the soul will not offer openly, freely and intimately to God, whether power, intelligence, knowledge or will. The individual acknowledges not only sin but the goodness of God. It is a great indication of love when someone tells God that He is good. David often mentions this confession in his psalms when he says: "Let the Lord know that He is good."

Now I have spoken about four sons of Leah. After that

she left off bearing children for a time. In the same way a human soul thinks that it has all it needs when it feels that it loves the real goodness of God. That is enough for salvation, but not for perfection, for the perfect soul has both to be inflamed with the fire of love in the affection and illumined with the light of knowledge in the rational mind.

Richard of St Victor

8. *The Interior Temple*

Use your body for the glory of God.

The hermit will never read the following words of St Paul without experiencing a thrill of joy:

"Don't you realize that you are God's temple and that the Holy Spirit is living inside you? . . . God's temple is sacred, and you are that temple."

"Don't you realize that your body is the temple of the Holy Spirit who is inside you and comes to you from God? That is why you should use your body for the glory of God."

Do not look for God in place or space. Close the eyes of your body, chain up your imagination and go down into yourself: you reach the Holy of Holies where the Holy Spirit dwells.

The moment you were baptized, you became the temple of God: "I baptize you in the name of the Father and of the Son and of the Holy Spirit." "Forthwith, the love of God was poured into your heart by the Holy Spirit, which was then given to you", in fulfilment of Jesus's promise:

"If anyone loves me," that is to say, if he has charity, if he is in a state of grace, "my Father will love him, and We shall come to him and make our home with him."

You know what this presence means: something quite

different from the Creator's presence in His creature. By it, you contract a divine friendship, inducting you into an intimate relationship with the Trinity, now your guest. The hermit sees this indwelling presence of God as the specific personal reason for withdrawing into the desert. He comes here to live this divine truth, to the exclusion of all other occupation. In this, above all, his vocation is an eschatological one: he begins, on earth, in the shadows of faith, by the light of love, what he will be doing for all eternity, where there will only be one temple: God Himself. Isn't he already more in God than God in him, by virtue of his willing ascent to the very secret mystery of the relationships between the Father, the Son and the Holy Spirit?

Man is contemplative both by destiny and by nature:

"Eternal life is this", Jesus teaches: "to know You, the only true God, and Jesus Christ whom You have sent."

But to know this with an awareness participating in God's own awareness, seeing him face to face in the beatific vision. To know him is the supreme objective of our minds, which are made for truth. To love Him is the sum of our will, which is greedy for the Good. Our earthly condition interposes a whole gamut of partial truths and fragmentary goods between God and us and, although these ought to help us to return to their source, as often as not they divert us from it by reason of the undue value which we place on them.

Isn't it strange that man, designed to flourish in contemplation dilating him to the proportions of God, should prefer activities which throw him back on himself in his will-to-achieve? It is easier to act than to pray: here the initiative belongs to God, there it is our own, and we do not enjoy giving our freedom up — even for the Lord's benefit. This presents a real puzzle to faith: that most people dislike contemplation and regard it as the idle Christian's pastime.

Indifference to God's presence in the soul is an insult, and sin a sort of sacrilege:

If anyone destroys the temple of God,
  God will destroy him.

The hermit has abandoned everything to become fixed in
this presence. With all earthly avenues closed, he dares
advance his claim to be a "fellow-citizen with the saints".
His Christian profession and formal vocation summoning
him to solitude are the basis for his claim. There, if he
understands it aright, there is only one temple, body and
soul. The disciplining of his senses and the "enslavement of
his flesh" will take on a higher meaning than that of a
laboriously sustained effort of self-mastery; the body, for
its part, is a valuable stone which must be cut and polished
to form part of the Church now in process of being built.
Far from debasing it, the hermit will treat it with respect,
mindful of the role assigned to it by the liturgy. The liturgy
lays down a detailed ritual, governing and ennobling the
attitudes and functions of each limb in the way it should
play its part in prayer and sacrifice.

The dignity of the body is primarily derived from the
soul which animates it, substantial union with which
allows it to share the honour of being the dwelling-place of
the Most High. Our more enlightened theology of the body
no longer permits us to treat it in the squalid way affected
by the hermits of old. Baptism has washed it in purifying
water, the priest has signed it with the Cross and anointed
it with holy chrism, and eucharistic communion makes it a
living ciborium. When it dies, the Church censes it and
carries it in triumph. For isn't it the "temple of the Holy
Spirit"?

Act then, so that it becomes what it is. Thanks to the
proper functioning of its organs, the body makes it possible
for the soul consciously to enjoy the presence of God
within her. Be careful that indiscreet severity does not
make you unable to maintain your prolonged conversation
with the Lord within you. If Mary Magdalen had been

suffering from migraine, the conversation at Bethany would have been spoilt.

You cannot consider what is taking place inside you, without a sense of joy. While you are eating, while you are relaxing, while you are asleep, the Father is begetting His Divine Son in your soul. His word is coming true every second: "Today I have begotten you."

Try by faith to perceive something of these exchanges of love and praise between the Divine Persons, for of such is the life and glory of the Trinity now irradiating your own soul.

The *Gloria Patri* punctuating your psalmody is only an echo, though a most faithful one, of the praise which Father, Son and Holy Spirit render to one another.

The Father's glory is His Son, receiving and perfectly reflecting all His perfections. He is His inward Word, His song. He praises Him as the source of all divine excellences, the "beginning".

The Son's glory is the Father, bearing witness, while begetting Him as perfect as Himself, to His transcendent beauty.

The Holy Spirit's glory is the mutual joy of the Father and the Son, whose substantial kiss He is.

Ask Him to let you be more sensitive to this magnificent hymn, summing up all other religious acts, that is to say, every act of your hermit-life, since all are directed to glorifying God.

As you repeat this ineffable *Gloria* with the Trinity, you share the Trinity's bliss. This is the supreme consolation the desert can offer, and the only one the hermit may legitimately covet. For one drop of this gladness, the saints have forsaken everything. In your retreat, try to put your heart in tune with God's heart, so that your joy consists in whatever gives joy to each of the Divine Persons.

The Father's joy is His Son. And is entirely expressed in the begetting word:

Filius meus es tu . . . "You are my son."

— the Word like Him in all respects, His living image, to whom He is drawn in all love and who returns that love in equal degree.

The Son's joy is His Father, from whom He receives all that He is: the Father who at a stroke transfers all His fruitfulness to Him, sharing His divine nature with Him and all His own perfections; the Son's bliss it is to be "nearest to the Father's heart" and to love Him with infinite gratitude super-added.

The Holy Spirit's joy is the very joy of Father and Son fusing together in this third person. Being the substantial love of the first two persons, the Holy Spirit is called the heart of God. He is a song, divine festival, the sublime vibrancy of Love. In God, He is the hearth of joy and bliss.

No human joy can compare with the bliss of the Godhead. But the hermit knows that this is not some alien wonder, still less a proposition to be worked out from books, not a distant spectacle, the inaccessible splendour of which would only make his own Thebaid the more dismal.

Temple of the Godhead, the heart of God beats in you. In the heart of your soul, the marvellous life of the Trinity is taking place. Remember these words of a theologian:

At this very moment, which I am wasting on trifles, Almighty God is busy within me, bringing His Co-eternal Son to birth.

You are God's adopted child and hence you live in the bosom of the divine family, where Jesus sponsors you and trains you:

Father, I want those whom you have given Me to be with Me where I am.

And where is Jesus? "In the Father's bosom." Faith, charity and sharing in the awareness which God has of Himself, in the love which He bears to Himself, plunge you into the living current of circumincession. Isn't that the meaning of Christ's prayer:

> That they may be one as we are one,
>   I in them and you in me.

This, then, will be your interior life in the hermitage: as continuously as you can, you will associate your personal acts with the three Divine Persons' song of glory and love, so that your own acts, assumed by Jesus Christ, may rise, infinitely precious, to God. Depending on the dictates of the moment, unite with the Father in celebrating the glory of the Son, with the Son in exalting the glory of the Father, with the Holy Spirit in tasting the joy of the Trinity entire.

This can only be consistently done in lively faith, bareness of mind and silence. No creature, no image will help you. Though created things reveal God's nature to you, they tell you nothing about the way He lives. To grasp this, you must go beyond terrestrial things and forget them. The day when you feel a genuine desire forcing you to sigh:

> Like a doe crying out
>   for running water,
> my soul cries aloud
>   for you, O God.
> My soul is thirsty for God,
>   O living God

you will know that God is knocking at your door and wants to "share your meal". That will be the Spirit of the Son, whom God has sent into your heart, crying "Abba, Father", and with ineffable groans begging on your behalf for "those things which are according to the mind of God", which for you means perfect union with Him.

Such is the last why and wherefore of the hermit's

detachment: why he follows the Lord's advice to the letter, "by retiring into his cells, shutting the door and praying to his Father, who is there in that secret place". He does this physically, and even more so spiritually, by intense recollectedness in the interior cell which the hermitage affords him.

Have no scruples about only devoting little time to "devotions", about not overloading yourself with particular intentions: the official prayer of the Church provides for all, and the honour which the Church renders to the saints in her offices and the apostolic efficacity of her supplication, far exceed any private homage or intercession of yours. Jesus in heaven, says the Epistle to the Hebrews, "is living forever to intercede on your behalf". He does this, not by formulated requests, but by the sole presence of the glorious scars of His passion: the reminders of His love and obedience. By virtue of its consecrated state and fervent charity, your whole existence pleads that God's name should be hallowed, that His Kingdom should come and that His will be done.

The hermit may rightly consider himself as already taking part in the glorious liturgy of eternity, described in Revelation. He already has his place among the myriads of myriads, among the thousands of thousands of angels and saints assembled round the throne of God, "shouting: to the One who is sitting on the throne and to the Lamb, be all praise, honour, glory and power for ever and ever."

If your liturgy is made as simple as it can be, if you are allowed long hours of solitude and leisure, this is to let your soul, set free of all constraints, anticipate as far as may be what our eternal life will be. For all this, do not hope never again to experience the heaviness and boredom of desolate prayer. The festival is all for faith and love. The joy is God's, not yours – as regards what is felt.

However unhappy you may be, adoration – for egoism can play no part in this – will always be a blessed release for you from self-concern. God's bliss will be your joy: this is the supreme disinterestedness of true charity.

May the lovely acclamations of the *Gloria in excelsis* ring out unceasingly in the temple of your soul:

> Glory to God in highest Heaven . . .
> We praise You, we bless You,
> we adore You, we glorify You,
> and we give You thanks
> for Your immense glory . . .

Since no other voice is raised in the desert but yours, at least there will be one place on earth where God is worshipped purely . . .

*A Cistercian
to a Novice*

9. *Holiness Possible Everywhere*

I can hardly recall all that I said last Sunday. My general impression is that I told you two things: first, that we are bound to seek our sanctification in that state wherein Providence has placed us, rather than to build castles in the air concerning great possible virtue in positions we do not fill; and secondly that we need very diligent faithfulness to God in the smallest things.

Most people spend the best part of their life in avowing and regretting their habits, in talking about changing them; in making rules for a future time which they look for, but which is not given them; and in thereby losing time which ought to be spent in good works and in setting forward their salvation.

You should treat all such notions as very dangerous. Our salvation ought to be the work of every day and every hour. No time is fitter for it than that which God in His

Mercy accords us now; and that because today is ours, but we know not what tomorrow may bring forth. Salvation is not to be achieved by wishing for it, but by seeking it heartily. The uncertainty of life ought to make us realize that we should prosecute this undertaking with all our energies, and that all other pursuits are worthless, since they do not bring us nearer to God, the rightful End of all we do – the God of our salvation, as David continually calls Him in the Psalms.

Why do we make plans for advancing in perfection? Because we believe it necessary to our salvation. Why, then, do we defer carrying them out, when it is just as necessary to seek now after salvation as it will be ten years hence; now at court, as hereafter in a more retired life? Surely it is wise always to take the safest side in whatever concerns salvation, a matter in which we lose all or gain all. That state of life to which God has called us is safe for us so long as we fulfil all our duties therein. If God foresaw that it was impossible to be saved at court, He would have forbidden us to live in it. But so far from this, He has appointed kings and their courts, and gives men that birth and position which admits them to those courts. So we may be sure that it is His Will that souls at court should be saved, and find the narrow way to Heaven, the way of truth, that way which Jesus Christ has said "shall make us free" (John 8:32) – in other words, shall guide us out of all the dangers to which the world exposes us.

And so much the more you meet with these dangers in your present state of life, so much the more you must keep watch over yourself, that you yield not to them. Keeping watch over self means hearkening to God; it means always abiding in His Presence, being always recollected, never plunging into voluntary dissipation or distraction amid the things of this world; it means as far as possible caring for retirement, prayer, and good books; it means what David calls "pouring out your heart before God" (Psalm 62:8), feeling Him within you, seeking Him earnestly, loving Him above all else, avoiding whatever is displeasing to Him. Such goodness as this is suitable to every state of life; it will be most helpful to any one living at court, and I know nothing better adapted to teach you to be in the world without being of the world. Pray adopt it, and strive never to forget that you are with God and He with you, so that you may abide steadfast in His service.

Make a habit of frequently adoring His Holy Will by humbly submitting yourself to the order of His Good Providence. Ask Him to uphold you, lest you fall. Intreat Him to perfect His work in you, so that, having inspired you in your present state of life with the desire to be saved, you may actually work out your salvation therein. He does not require great things for success. Our Lord Himself has said, "The Kingdom of God is within you" (Luke 17:21); we can find it there when we will. Let us do what we know He requires of us, and so soon as we perceive His Will in anything, let there be no drawing back, only absolute faithfulness. Such faithfulness ought not merely to lead us to do great things for His service and for our salvation, but whatever our hand finds to do, or which appertains to our state of life. If one could only be saved by means of great deeds but few could hope for salvation. It depends, however, in fulfilling God's Will. The smallest things become great when God requires them of us. They are only small as regards themselves; but they forthwith become great when done for Him, when they lead to Him, and serve to unite with Him eternally.

Remember how He has said, "He that is faithful in that which is least is faithful also in much, and he that is unjust in the least is unjust also in much" (Luke 16:10). I should say that a soul which sincerely longs after God never considers whether a thing be small or great; it is enough to know that He for whom it is done is infinitely great, that it is His due to have all creation solely devoted to His Glory, which can only be by fulfilling His Will.

As to you, I think you should accept your crosses as your chief acts of penitence; the worries of the world ought to teach you to sit loose to it, and your weakness wean you from yourself. If you bear this continual burthen patiently, you cannot fail to advance in the narrow way. It is narrow by reason of the sorrows which wring your heart; but it is broad by reason of the enlargement God vouchsafes to that heart. One may suffer, be surrounded by contrarieties – one may even be deprived of spiritual consolations, yet be free because one accepts all suffering without seeking deliverance. One bears one's own weakness, preferring it to more agreeable conditions, because it is God's choice. The great thing is to suffer without losing courage.

François Fénelon

10. *Dryness in Devotion*

I have observed that you reckon rather overmuch upon your fervour and recollection: God has withdrawn these visible gifts to teach you detachment, that you may learn how weak you are of yourself, and to accustom you to serve Him without the conscious satisfaction which makes all service easy. We do Him a far more real service when the very same things are done without satisfaction and against the grain. It is a small service I render my friend, if, being fond of walking and possessing strong legs, I go to see him on foot; but if I am gouty and every step pains me, then those visits, on which heretofore my friend set no store, begin to have a new value; they become tokens of a very real and lively friendship: the more difficulty I have in paying them the more he will appreciate them, since one step is worth more than a mile once was! I do not say this to flatter you and fill you with self-confidence; God forbid!

but only to prevent your yielding to a very dangerous temptation, that of anxiety and depression. When you are full of warmth and fervour, think nothing of your good works, which do but flow spontaneously from the source. But, on the contrary, when you feel dry, dull, cold, almost helpless, then abide in patient faith under God's hand; confess your weakness, turn to His never-failing Love, and, above all, never mistrust His help. Be sure it is very profitable to the soul to feel stripped of all visible stay, and reduced to cry out, "In Thy Sight shall no man living be justified".

Persevere in your onward path, in God's Name, though you may feel as if you had not strength or courage to put one foot before the other. If human courage fails you, all the better; resignation to God will not fail you in your helplessness. St Paul said, "When I am weak then I am strong." And when he besought deliverance from his infirmity, God answered, "My strength is made perfect in weakness". Let yourself be perfected by the experience of your imperfection, and by humble recourse to Him who is the strength of the weak. Try quietly in your meditation to seek whatever will promote recollection; do not harass yourself. Soothe your imagination, which is one while excitable, the next exhausted: make use of whatever will tend to calm you and to promote a familiar loving communion with God. Whatever is most comforting to you in this way will be most profitable. "Where the Spirit of God is, there is liberty." Such liberty is to be found in simply following such leadings as draw you closest to the Beloved One. Your inner poverty will often recall the consciousness of your misery: God in His Goodness will not suffer you to lose sight of your own unworthiness, and that will speedily bring you back to His feet. Be of good cheer – God's work can only be done through self-renunciation. I pray that He would uphold, comfort, impoverish you, and teach you the full meaning of His own words, "Blessed are the poor in spirit".

François Fénelon

11. Desolation and Consolation

On the other hand, what if both these forms of evidence and all the things that support them as I have just listed them, once you have had some or all of them, start to disappear, and you seem barren, not only without your new ardency but also quite unable to carry out the spiritual exercises you are accustomed to. Well, then you're between the two: you haven't got either of them; you're without them both. But don't be too distressed about this. Instead you must put up with it in all humility and await patiently what the Lord decides. It seems to me that you are on a spiritual sea, voyaging from an active to a contemplative condition. It is possible for great storms and temptations to assail you during such a transition stage, and you won't know where to get help. It will seem to you that you have lost everything, the usual as well as the unusual graces. All the same, you mustn't be too distressed, even though there seems every ground for a feeling of desolation. Instead trust lovingly in our Lord, as much as your state allows you, even though that may not be much. He isn't very far away. He will look at you again, very soon perhaps, and touch you with that same grace more powerfully than you have ever felt it before. Then you will think that you are quite healthy again in every way. But only for a while. All of a sudden, almost before you know where you are, it will all be over again and you will be knocked down in your vessel, with that feeling of barrenness and being blown hither and thither, you just don't know where.

Don't worry. I assure you that He will come again, as soon as He decides to, and will take you out of that desolate state, releasing you from all your distress and worry, far more effectively than ever in the past. You just have to remember that whenever He departs, it won't be too long before He returns. And whenever He returns, He will do so more wonderfully and powerfully and joyfully than ever before, if you will only last out patiently. His intention, you see, is to make you fit His will spiritually, as closely as a fine French leather glove fits your own hand.

Since He sometimes goes and sometimes comes, it is obvious that in so doing He wants to test you secretly and to train you for the exercise you have undertaken. He is testing your patience, to see if it is up to the task. That is why He takes your feeling of ardency away from you. That is all it is. You think He has gone away but it's only your fervour. Look at it this way: even though God sometimes takes away these sweet feelings, and ardent, even burning desires, He never removes His graces from those He loves. It is more than I can believe that He could ever remove His special grace from His chosen ones, once He has given it to them, unless they commit a mortal sin. But those feelings of sweetness, ardency and burning desire are not in themselves grace. They are merely outward signs of grace. God often takes them away to try our patience, and in order to help us spiritually in many other ways that we just don't understand. Grace itself is something so elevated, pure and spiritual that our senses are incapable of appreciating it. We can see or feel its outward signs, but not grace itself. So our Lord will sometimes take away your feelings of ardency in order to toughen and purify your patience, though not just for that reason – there are many others which I haven't time to go into here. But I must get back to my main point.

What you imagine is God's presence but isn't actually – the character, frequency and increasing intensity of the physical consolations I have spoken of – is something He uses to feed and strengthen your spirit so that you can live and keep on living in His service and in love of Him. If you

are patient when He takes away those outward consolations, or outward signs of grace, and if your spirit is
profoundly fed and lovingly strengthened when He allows
you to feel them, it is because He wants you both in
consolation and in desolation to be eager for and perfectly
moulded for perfection and spiritual union with His own
will. Such is a union of perfect love. When you do enter
such a union, you will be as delighted and pleased to go
without those physical consolations (if that's what He
wants) as you would be to have and experience them
continuously throughout your whole life.

When you are in this condition, your love is chaste and
perfect. You see your God and see your love for Him at the
same time. You also experience Him directly as He is in
Himself, at the highest level of your spirit, in being spiritually united with His love. But don't forget that this
experience is unseeing in the usual sense. It can't be anything else on this earth. You are wholly without your own
self. You are naked but you are clothed in God, as God is
clothed in God. When I say that you are unclothed, I mean
that you are naked of those physical consolations which
you experience in this earthly life, however pleasurable or
holy they are. You can perceive and feel God, truly and
absolutely; as He is in Himself, only in a pure spirit; and a
pure spirit is something quite unlike any image of the mind
or false idea we might happen to dream up in this life.

You cannot separate the sight and feeling of God as He
is in Himself, seen and felt in the mind of the person seeing
and experiencing Him thus, from God's own being, any
more than God Himself can be separated from His own
being. God's own self and God's own existence are one,
substantially and in nature. God cannot be separated from
His existence by reason of any kind of natural union.
Similarly, the soul that perceives and feels God as I have
described Him cannot be separated from what it perceives
and feels, because it is joined in grace with God.

It will now be apparent how through these outward signs you will to some degree be able to experience, and even to some extent to test, the orientation and profound character of your vocation, and how grace is guiding you, inwardly through your spiritual exercises and outwardly through reading or listening to advice about it all. Then, whenever you or anyone with the same spiritual inclination and development has in some way truly experienced all these, or one or two of these signs (though so very few people have the special experience of this grace that from the start enables them, immediately or almost immediately, to test them all out authentically – though one may not experience them all at once initially it is enough to experience one or two of them); and if the true testimony of the Bible, your spiritual director and your own conscience agree, then for a while you can stop speculative meditation, and imagining the characteristics of your own being and God's, and of your own and God's behaviour. You have fed your mental abilities with such meditations, and they helped you to proceed from a worldly life and a wholly earthly existence to the state of grace in which you now find yourself. Now is the time for you to learn how to exercise yourself spiritually, in consciousness of yourself and of God, whom in times past you learned to understand so well from active thinking and imagining.

The Author of
The Cloud of Unknowing

12. *Contemplation in the Streets*

At this point, my friend, I am sure there is a question in your mind, accompanied by a slight smile.

"Well, then! Is there no value in action, duty to our fellow men, plunging oneself like leaven into this secular city? Must we all go into the desert? Is that possible? The desert is far away, I shall never be able . . ."

I know that's what you were thinking, and I must explain myself quite clearly, because something really crucial is at stake.

Charles de Foucauld said one day: "If the contemplative life were possible only behind convent walls or in the silence of the desert we should, in fairness, give a little convent to every mother of a family, and a track of desert to every person working hard in a bustling city to earn his living."

The vision of the reality in which the majority of poor men live determined the central crisis of his life; the crisis which was to carry him far from his first understanding of the religious life.

As you may know, Charles de Foucauld was a Trappist, and had chosen the poorest Trappist monastery in existence, that of Akbès in Syria. One day his superior sent him to watch by the corpse of a Christian Arab who had died in a poor house.

When Brother Charles was in the dead man's hovel he saw real poverty around him: hungry children and a weak, defenceless widow without assurance of the next day's bread. It was this spiritual crisis which was to make him leave La Trappe and go in search of a religious life very different from the earlier one.

"We, who have chosen the imitation of Jesus and Jesus Crucified, are very far from the trials, the pains, the insecurity and the poverty to which these people are subjected.

"I no longer want a monastery which is too secure. I want a small monastery, like the house of a poor workman who is not sure if tomorrow he will find work and bread, who with all his being shares the suffering of the world.

"Oh, Jesus, a monastery like your house at Nazareth, in which to live hidden as you did when you came among us."

When he came out of La Trappe, Foucauld founded his first fraternity at Beni-Abbès in the Sahara; later he built his hermitage at Tamanrasset where he died, murdered by the Tuareg.

The fraternity was to resemble the house of Nazareth, a house just like one of the many houses one sees along the many streets of the world.

Had he renounced contemplation then? Had his fervid spirit of prayer weakened? No, he had taken a step forward. He had decided to live the contemplative life along the streets, in a situation similiar to that of any ordinary man.

That step is much harder!

It is a step that God wants mankind to make.

The life of Charles de Foucauld opens up a new understanding of the spiritual life in which many will force themselves to make the fusion between contemplation and action – really living and obeying the first commandment of the Lord, "Love God above all things and your neighbour as yourself."

"Contemplation in the streets." This is tomorrow's task not only for the Little Brothers, but for all the poor.

Let us begin to analyse this element of "desert" which must be present, especially today, in the carrying out of such a demanding programme.

When one speaks of the soul's desert, and says that the desert must be present in your life, you must not think only of the Sahara or the desert of Judea, or into the High Valley of the Nile.

Certainly it is not everyone who can have the advantage of being able to carry out in practice this detachment from daily life. The Lord conducted me into the real desert because I was so thick skinned. For *me*, it was necessary. But all that sand was not enough to erase the dirt from my soul, even the fire was not enough to remove the rust from Ezekiel's pot.

113

But the same way is not for everybody. And if you cannot go into the desert, you must none the less "make some desert" in your life. Every now and then leaving men and looking for solitude to restore, in prolonged silence and prayer, the stuff of your soul. This is the meaning of "desert" in your spiritual life.

One hour a day, one day a month, eight days a year, for longer if necessary, you must leave everything and everybody and retire, alone with God. If you don't look for this solitude, if you don't love it, you won't achieve real contemplative prayer. If you are able to do so but nevertheless do not withdraw in order to enjoy intimacy with God, the fundamental element of the relationship with the All-Powerful is lacking: love. And without love no revelation is possible.

But the desert is not the final stopping place. It is a stage on the journey. Because, as I told you, our vocation is contemplation in the streets.

For me, this is quite costly. The desire to continue living here in the Sahara for ever is so strong that I am already suffering in anticipation of the order that will certainly come from my superiors: "Brother Charles, leave for Marseilles, leave for Morocco, leave for Venezuela, leave for Detroit.

"You must go back among men, mix with them, live your intimacy with God in the noise of their cities. It will be difficult but you must do it. And for this the grace of God will not fail you.

"Every morning, after Mass and meditation, you will make your way to work in a store or shipyard. And when you get back in the evening, tired, like all poor men forced to earn their living, you will enter the little chapel of the brotherhood and remain for a long time in adoration; bringing to your prayer all that world of suffering, of darkness, and often of sin, in the midst of which you have lived for eight hours taking your share of pain and toil."

Contemplation in the streets. A good phrase, but very demanding.

Carlo Carretto

13. The Solitary Soul

*He has taken me into his cellar
and the banner he raises over me
is love.*

Of all these splendours, the first weeks in your cell will reveal very little, perhaps nothing. Humbly accept the boredom, the pacing to and fro. Your heart is still raw from everything which you have left behind, and the whitewashed walls are bare except for a crucifix and a madonna. There is still too much tumult in your imagination and emotions for you to be enthralled by the Invisible. You used to dream of this little house, sister to the one (it would seem) where the *Imitation of Christ* was written. Now you are in it and you shudder. You would like to run away.

Be patient, pray, quickly devise a round of activities, reading, short studies in the Bible or any other spiritual subject which attracts you. You will gradually discover and come to savour the delights of the cell. Those who have celebrated these in moving phrases echoing down the centuries were not novices, believe me, and like you had first experienced its austerity.

The hermit's cell is a dwelling unique of its kind. It is neither a clergyman's office, nor the cell of a Jesuit or a mendicant. The solitary sleeps in it, works in it, eats and relaxes in it. But its distinguishing characteristic is that it is his entire universe. Apart from his visits to the church, he must seek nothing outside it. For him, everything is contained within this minute enclosure.

All the riches of the desert, of the mountain and of the

temple are so concentrated for the hermit here that if he leaves without some reason dictated by obedience, he instantly loses all. He finds nothing outside; what nourishes other people's piety is of no use to him. The hermit is tied to his cell for his soul's subsistence.

The cell is a shelter from the miasmas of the world, a holy place where the Lord pays secret visits to the soul and where the soul waits in recollectedness for Him, having scorned all else. It is the "wine cellar" into which He takes His beloved, to make her drunk with His presence and His presents.

It would be a profanation to abandon yourself to futile activities there. There God grants audience to the solitary soul. On the confines of earthly life, released from those contingencies under which most souls athirst for God must groan since victims of life's harsh conditions, the hermit begins his eternity rejoicing in the Lord.

If you are generous, little by little you will see the divine world emerging from the shadows. You have been living in it unawares, the hurly-burly of the world not having allowed it to be seen. You then in your turn will wonderingly discover that you are never less alone than when you are alone . . .

A Cistercian
to a Novice

5

Encountering Darkness

1. Tribulations

We know not what to pray for as we ought in regard to tribulations, which may do us good or harm; and yet, because they are hard and painful, and against the natural feelings of our weak nature, we pray, with a desire which is common to mankind, that they may be removed from us. But we ought to exercise such submission to the will of the Lord our God, that if He does not remove those vexations, we do not suppose ourselves to be neglected by Him, but rather, in patient endurance of evil, hope to be made partakers of greater good, for so His strength is perfected in our weakness. God has sometimes in anger granted the request of impatient petitioners, as in mercy He denied it to the apostle. For we read what the Israelites asked, and in what manner they asked and obtained their request; but while their desire was granted, their impatience was severely corrected (Numbers 11). Again, He gave them, in answer to their request, a king according to their heart, as it is written, not according to His own heart (1 Samuel 8:6, 7). He granted also what the devil asked, namely, that His servant, who was to be proved, might be tempted (Job 1:12, 2:6). He granted also the request of unclean spirits, when they besought Him that their legion might be sent into the great herd of swine (Luke 8:32). These things are written to prevent any one from thinking too highly of himself if he has received an answer when he was urgently asking anything which it would be more advantageous for him not to receive, or to prevent him from being cast down and despairing of the divine compassion towards himself if he be not heard, when, perchance, he is asking something by the obtaining of which he might be more grievously

119

afflicted, or might be by the corrupting influences of prosperity wholly destroyed. In regard to such things, therefore, we know not what to pray for as we ought. Accordingly, if anything is ordered in a way contrary to our prayer, we ought, patiently bearing the disappointment, and in everything giving thanks to God, to entertain no doubt whatever that it was right that the will of God and not our will should be done. For of this the Mediator has given us an example, inasmuch as, after He had said, "Father, if it be possible, let this cup pass from me", transforming the human will which was in Him through His incarnation, He immediately added, "Nevertheless, O Father, not as I will but as Thou wilt." Wherefore, not without reason are many made righteous by the obedience of One.

> *St Augustine*
> *to Proba*

2. To One in Great Trouble

Everything combines to try you; but God, who loves you, will not suffer you to be tried above that you are able to bear. He will use the trials for your progress. Still you must not pry curiously even into this, but remember that God's hand is none the less powerful when it is invisible. His workings are for the most part out of sight: we should never really die to self if we always saw His hand visibly succouring us. At that rate He would sanctify us amid life, and all spiritual gifts; not in crosses, darkness, privation, death. Our dear Lord did not say, "If any one will come after Me, let him be richly clothed, let him be satiate with delights, like St Peter on Mount Tabor, let him rejoice in himself and in Me, and trust to his spiritual perfection." No; He said, "If any one will come after Me, this is the road by which he must pass : he must renounce himself, he must take up his cross and follow Me, along the edge of precipices which seem to bristle with death." St Paul speaks of our craving to be "clothed upon", but before we are so clothed by Jesus Christ we must be "unclothed" (2 Corinthians 5:4).

So then let yourself be stripped of all to which self clings, the better to receive that robe made white in the Blood of the Lamb, which has no purity save His own. Happy the soul which has nothing of its own, and shines solely through His light. O bride, never so beautiful as when without ornament of thine own, as when wholly His!

Remember that the great seducer of all is "I" : it seduces more souls than even Eve's tempter the serpent! Blessed is that soul which listens so devoutly to God's voice as to forget to heed and pity self!

I would that I could be with you, but God does not suffer it. Or say rather that God brings us much nearer in Himself, the Centre of all that are His, than if we were in the same place. I am near you in spirit, I share your trials and your languor. . . . But you must die to yourself in order that Christ may live in you.

François Fénelon

3. On Suffering

7 October 1921

You bring up, my child, a point which I suppose you really feel an objection. Even if you do not feel it so, I think it well worthwhile to clear out this corner of your mind, so as to make quite sure that you correctly seize the truly great doctrine of Purgatory. I want, then, to make sure that you clearly understand that, according to that doctrine, suffering (*rightly accepted* suffering) is indeed usually necessary for, is inherent in, the Purification from sin, evil habits, etc. But it makes no substantial distinction between such Purification as taking place already here, or taking place in the Beyond. In all our Retreats we are taught that it will have been our own fault, if the sufferings of our life here have not sufficed to purify us from our sins and evil habits. Of course, even very great sufferings would not, simply of themselves, purify us from even small evil habits. It is only suffering *meekly accepted, willed, transfigured by love of God, of Christ* – it is only such, that will purify or cure anything. This is so true that, where the love is perfect, this *love alone, without any suffering* not directly prompted by itself, completely blots out the evil dispositions. Such a soul, even if previously a great sinner, goes straight to Heaven upon its death. Yes, in all cases, Purgatory applies indifferently to suffering rightly borne in *this* life and the same similarly borne in *that* life. There is simply no such thing, as a Purgatory hereafter. On the contrary, every pang God allows to reach us here, and which we manage to bear a little well, does *a work not to be repeated*. We become thus fitter and fitter for complete union with Christ and God from the very minute of our death.

I have written "a little well" on purpose. For to suffer well is far more difficult than to act well (although the ordinary talk is that we have just "to grin and bear" suffering – we can do nothing to it or with it!!!) Holy suffering is the very crown of holy action. And God is no pedant: He can and does look to the substance of our suffering, and knows how to penetrate beyond our surface restlessness or murmurs. Indeed, part of the great work suffering effects in the soul doubtless springs from the way in which, when acute, it almost invariably humbles us: we can much less easily cut a fine figure in our own eyes over our sufferings, than we can over our actions when in peace and plenty.

You understand all the above completely, I trust? We will both do what gently, peaceably we can to have all our Purgatory – every drop of it – here; and then Heaven, the closest union, unfailing, with Pure Joy, with All Purity, with Christ, with God.

Baron Friedrich von Hügel
to his Niece

4. Riding the Storm

June 404

To the most worthy deaconess, beloved of God, Olympias, John the Bishop sends greetings in the Lord.

Come now, I am going to ease the soreness of your despondency and scatter the thoughts which have given rise to this sombre cloud. What bewilders your mind, why do you grieve and torment yourself? Because the storm that has rushed upon the churches is fierce and threatening, because it has shrouded all in moonless darkness and is working up to a crisis, day after day bringing cruel shipwreck while the whole world is toppling over into ruin? I am aware of this too; there is no one to deny it. Whenever you hear that one of the churches has been submerged, another tossed in dire distress, this one drowned by the angry flood, that mortally injured in some way, that a certain church has received a wolf instead of a shepherd, a second a pirate instead of a helmsman, a third an executioner instead of a physician, be saddened by all means, for one ought not to endure such things without pain. But since grieve you must, at the same time set a limit to your sorrow. If you like, I will sketch the present position for you to depict the tragedy in even clearer lines.

We see the ocean upheaved from its very bed, we see the

dead bodies of sailors floating on the surface, others over-whelmed by the waves, ships' decks split asunder, sails rent, masts broken in pieces, the oars slipped out of the hands of the rowers, the helmsmen sitting idle on the decks opposite their tillers, hands folded on knees. Before the hopelessness of the situation they can only groan aloud, utter piercing shrieks, wail, lament. No sky visible, no sea: everything lies in deep, obscure and gloomy darkness; no man can descry his neighbour. The roaring waves swell and thunder, sea beasts rise on every side to threaten the voyagers. Why try to find words for what cannot be expressed? For whatever simile I choose for present-day evils, words elude and fail me altogether.

I am conscious of these disasters, yet for all that I do not relinquish a most firm hope. I keep my mind fixed on the Pilot of all things; He does not ride the storm by steersmanship, but by a mere nod He breaks the surging of the sea, and if not immediately, if not at once, that precisely is His way. He does not cut calamities short at the outset, but averts them only as they approach their climax when almost all have abandoned hope. Only then does He show forth wonders and miracles and display that power which is His alone, while He schools the sufferers in patience.

Do not lose heart then. There is only one thing to be feared, Olympias, only one trial, and that is sin. I have told you this over and over again. All the rest is beside the point, whether you talk of plots, feuds, betrayals, slanders, abuses, accusations, confiscation of property, exile, sharpened swords, open sea or universal war. Whatever they may be, they are all fugitive and perishable. They touch the mortal body but wreak no harm on the watchful soul. Hence when blessed Paul wanted to stress the insignificance of earthly weal and woe, he summed it up in a single phrase: "The things that are seen are temporal" (2 Corinthians 4: 18). Why then fear the things that are temporal which will roll on in an ever-flowing stream? Whether pleasant or painful, the present does not last for ever.

Do not be perturbed therefore by all that is going on. Give up crying for help to this person or that and chasing shadows – for such is all human endeavour. Rather should you incessantly invoke Jesus whom you adore, that He may but turn His face towards you. Then, in one decisive moment, all your trouble is ended.

St John Chrysostom

5. *The Sweet and the Bitter*

God knows best what is needful for us, and all that He does is for our good. If we know how much He loves us, we should always be ready to receive equally and with indifference from His hand the sweet and the bitter. All would please that came from Him.

The sorest afflictions never appear intolerable, except when we see them in the wrong light. When we see them as dispensed by the hand of God, when we know that it is our loving Father who abuses and distresses us, our sufferings lose all their bitterness and our mourning becomes all joy.

Let our business be to know God; the more one knows Him, the more one desires to know Him. And as knowledge is commonly the measure of love, the deeper and more extensive our knowledge shall be, the greater will be our love; and if our love of God be great, we shall love Him equally in grief and in joy.

Brother Lawrence

6. *Sorrows and their Purpose*

Christ is in our midst!

In your last letter you told of having the same experiences again. But now, thank the Lord, they are over. If there were no sorrows, neither would there be salvation, said the Holy Fathers. Sorrows have two uses: the first is zeal towards God and whole-hearted thankfulness. The second is being delivered from vain cares and concerns. It is clear from the writings of the Holy Fathers that they too, like us, became depressed and faint-hearted, and they even went through experiences that they did not want to commit to writing lest they should disturb those of us who were inexperienced in the spiritual life and bring us to despair. Of course, the Lord permits sorrows in accordance with our powers, in the amount that each can bear. These trials humble us. We have a kind of self-confidence, we want to succeed in the spiritual life by our own powers, and it is in such sorrows that we learn humility, that our efforts cannot achieve their aims without God's help. Ours should be the effort towards virtue, but success even in virtue depends on grace, and grace is given by God and only to the humble. No one becomes humble without humbling events.

The wise spiritual life was explained with precision by the Holy Fathers in their writings, but what they wrote can best be understood by being lived. If you yourself work to free your heart of passions, then everything will be clearer and more understandable. Holy Fathers, pray to God for us sinners, and open our small minds to comprehend your writings.

You write that your duties distract you from prayer. As you work, keep the memory of God; this too is prayer. It is good that you have this striving for the spiritual life and for prayer. This is already half of salvation, and God will help you to go further. Only do not be depressed and faint-hearted; may the Lord help you.

You also write that you have not even reached a beginning. This feeling is a good thing; it leads to humility. According to the law of spiritual knowledge, spiritual life has to be like this. The closer a man comes to God, the more he sees his faults and his sinfulness. Lord, deliver man from seeing himself as righteous. May the Lord help you and save you from eternal suffering.

Staretz John

7. *A Rebellious Nature*

About the end of 1619

I see clearly this ant's nest of inclinations which self-love nourishes and pours over your heart, my dear daughter, and I am well aware that the nature of your mind, subtle, delicate, and fertile, contributes towards this; but still, my dear daughter, they are only inclinations, and since you feel their importunateness, and your heart complains of them, there is no appearance that they are accepted with any deliberate consent. No, my daughter; your dear soul having conceived the great desire with which God has inspired it of being His alone, do not easily yield to the thought that it gives consent to these contrary movements. Your heart may be shaken with the movement of these passions, but I think that it rarely sins by consenting.

Miserable man that I am, said the great Apostle (Romans 7: 24), *who shall deliver me from the body of this*

127

death? He felt within him an army composed of his natural humours, aversions, customs, and inclinations, which had conspired his spiritual death; and because he fears them he bears witness that he hates them, and because he hates them he cannot endure them without sorrow, and his sorrow makes him thus exclaim; to which he himself answers that *the grace of God by Jesus Christ* will defend him, not from the fear, not from the terror, not from the alarm, not from the fight, but from defeat, and will prevent him from being conquered.

My daughter, to be in the world and not feel these movements of the passions are incompatible things. Our glorious St Bernard says that it is heresy to say we can persevere in one same state here below, inasmuch as the Holy Spirit has said by Job (Job 14: 2), speaking of man, that *he never continueth in the same state.* This is in reply to what you say of the levity and inconstancy of your soul; for I believe firmly that that soul is continually agitated by the winds of its passions, and that consequently it is always shaking; but I firmly believe also that the grace of God and the resolution which it has given you remain continually at the pinnacle of your spirit, where the standard of the cross is ever upraised, and where faith, hope, and charity ever loudly proclaim – *Vive Jésus!*

You see, my daughter, these inclinations to pride, vanity, self-love, mingle themselves with everything, and sensibly or insensibly breathe their spirit into almost all our actions; but at the same time they are not the motives of our actions. St Bernard feeling them tease him one day while he was preaching said: "Depart from me, Satan; I did not begin for thee and I will not end for thee."

One thing only have I to say to you, my dear daughter, on your writing to me that you nourish your pride by little arts in conversations and in letters. In conversation, indeed, affectation sometimes enters so insensibly that one scarcely perceives it at all; but still if one does perceive it the style should immediately be altered; but in letters this is certainly a little less, yea much less, to be tolerated: for we see better what we are doing, and if we perceive a notable affectation we must punish the hand that wrote it, making it write another letter in other fashion.

For the rest, my dear daughter, I do not doubt but that amid so great a multitude of turnings and windings of the heart there glide in here and there some venial faults; but still, as they merely pass through, they do not deprive us of the fruit of our resolutions, but only of the sweetness which there would be in not making these failures, did the state of this life permit.

Well now, be just: do not excuse, no, nor accuse your poor soul save after mature consideration, for fear lest if you excuse it without foundation you make it presumptuous, and if you lightly accuse it you dull its spirit and make it low-hearted. Walk simply and you will walk confidently (Proverbs 10:9).

I must yet add on the remaining space of my paper this important word. Do not burden your weak body with any other austerity than that which the rule imposes on you; preserve your bodily strength to serve God with in spiritual exercises, which we are often obliged to give up, when we have indiscreetly overdone that with which the soul has to go through them.

Write to me when you please, without ceremony or fear; do not let respect oppose the love which God wills there should be between us, according to which I am for ever unchangeably your very humble brother and servant, &c.

St Francis de Sales
to the Abbess of Port Royal

8. *Spiritual Ordeals*

You know as well as I, dear Sister, that it is God's practice to make all souls, whom He wishes to raise to perfection, pass through every kind of interior tribulation and grief, that they may be tested, purified and detached from all things. The most painful of such tribulations are those which may be due to our own fault, and in which the poor soul, censured severely by itself, and still more severely by others, hears, either from within or without, only an answer that makes the heart sick unto death. The person of whom you have written to me is in this state. There is nothing to fear on her behalf; all the details you give me prove, on the contrary, that God has particular plans for her. When you write to her, speak only of patience, submission to God and utter self-abandonment to divine Providence, as you would to people in the world suffering from affliction and temporal adversity. Above all, let her try, by means of the most filial trust in God, to shun energetically avoidable anxieties. I use the word avoidable because the poor souls whom God subjects to this ordeal have no mastery of the griefs and anxieties which obsess them. These are the cause of their greatest sorrow, and the most grievous aspect of the state of humiliation in which God wills that for a certain time they shall remain. Then the one thing for them to do is to make submission to God in the matter of these paroxysms of interior grief as in all things else.

Tell this poor soul that her chief and almost continual prayer should be the silence she keeps at the foot of the cross of Jesus Christ, the while she murmurs, as once did He: "*Fiat*, not my will, O heavenly Father, but Yours be done in all things! It is You who shape all our afflictions for the good of our souls; all that You wish is for my greatest good and my eternal salvation; do with me, then, as it shall please You; I adore and I submit."

I consider that your friend does well not to examine her thoughts; such an examination would merely trouble her mind the more. Let her leave everything to God; let her despise those thoughts and those feigned outcries of conscience, and let her go forward without heeding them, at all times when there is nothing definitely wrong in the act she meditates performing. Such vain scruples are a temptation of the devil by which he robs her of peace and so hinders her from making progress in virtue, as a sick body, because of its weakness and languor, is incapable of manual labour.

When she succeeds in maintaining herself in this peace of the will, she will slowly recover, as a weak and languishing body recovers with rest and good food. I shall set down three methods of hastening her recovery: (1) She must put out of her mind everything that grieves and disquiets it, regarding this kind of thought as coming from the devil; for all that is of God is peaceful and gentle and agreeable, and serves only to strengthen trust in Him. It shares the peace in which He dwells, and in which He breeds those varied feelings of piety which leads souls to perfection. (2) She must constantly raise her mind and heart towards God, directing both mind and heart towards submission, self-abandonment and trust in that paternal goodness which at present afflicts, only to sanctify, her. (3) She must choose for her reading those books which can most powerfully contribute to bring her interior peace and inspire her with trust in God. These include Mgr Languet's treatise, the book entitled *Espérance chrétienne*, and St Francis de Sales's Letters. For the rest, let her go her own road, altering her conduct in no way, going to confession and holy communion as usual; for the devil, in order to deceive and still further weaken her, is quite capable of using all his cunning to inspire her with dislike and unto-ward fear of confession, communion and other spiritual exercises. She must lend no ear to such wicked inspirations, but as a good and true daughter of the Church at all times be guided by the light of faith and the blessed practices of the Christian religion. *Amen.*

Jean-Pierre de Caussade
to Sister Marie Anne Thérèse de Rosen

9. *Knowing God Before Loving Him*

Our good Sister . . . seems to me full of goodwill, but she wants to go faster than grace. One does not become holy all at once. I commend her to you.

I am filled with shame and confusion when I reflect, on the one hand, upon the great favours which God has bestowed and is still bestowing upon me; and, on the other, upon the ill use I have made of them, and my small advancement in the way of perfection.

We cannot escape the dangers which abound in life without the actual and continual help of God. Let us, then, pray to Him for it continually. How can we pray to Him without being with Him? How can we be with Him but in thinking of Him often? And how can we often think of Him unless by a holy habit of thought which we should form?

You will tell me that I am always saying the same thing. It is true, for this is the best and easiest method I know; and as I use no other, I advise all the world to do it.

We must know before we can love. In order to know God, we must often think of Him; and when we come to love Him we shall then also think of Him often, for our heart will be with our treasure.

Brother Lawrence

10. *Supported by Faith Alone*

At length I came insensibly to do the same thing during my set time of prayer, which caused in me great delight and consolation. This practice produced in me so high an esteem for God that faith alone was capable to satisfy me on that point.

Such was my beginning, and yet I must tell you that for the first ten years I suffered much. The apprehension that I was not devoted to God as I wished to be, my past sins always present to my mind, and the great unmerited favours which God bestowed on me, were the matter and source of my sufferings.

During this time I fell often, yet as often rose again. It seemed to me that all creation, reason, and God Himself were against me, and faith alone for me.

I was troubled sometimes with thoughts that to believe I had received such favours was an effect of my presumption, which pretended to be *at once* where others arrive only with difficulty; at other times that it was a wilful delusion, and that there was no salvation for me.

Brother Lawrence

11. *Faith, Our Support in Darkness*

God has many ways of drawing us to Himself. He sometimes hides Himself from us; but faith alone, which will not fail us in time of need, ought to be our support, and the foundations of our confidence, which must be all in God.

I know not how God will dispose of me. Happiness grows upon me. The whole world suffers; yet I, who deserve the severest discipline, feel joys so continual and so great that I can scarce contain them.

I would willingly ask of God a share of your sufferings, but that I know my weakness, which is so great that if He left me one moment to myself I should be the most wretched man alive. And yet I know not how He can leave me alone, because faith gives me as strong a conviction as sense can do that He never forsakes us until we have first forsaken Him.

Let us fear to leave Him. Let us be always with Him. Let us live and die in His presence. Do you pray for me as I for you.

Brother Lawrence

12. *Emptiness of Heart*

I thoroughly approve, dear Sister, of the patience with which you endure the great emptiness in your heart. As the result of it, you make greater progress in a single month than you would have done in several years of delight and consolation. In this matter I have only to exhort you to persist; for it is our essential need to cross this desert if during this life we are to reach the promised land.

I am not surprised that this great emptiness brings you strength. It does indeed, since God is present in it, although in a scarcely perceptible manner, no less than He is during spiritual ordeals. At all times look upon this general aversion, and apparent insensibility to all that is not of God, as a great grace. Carefully maintain yourself in this state of soul. At the moment indicated by His grace, God will come to fill that emptiness He now makes in your heart; while the ineffable sweetness with which His presence will be accompanied will arouse a new aversion in you for all this world's paltry satisfactions.

Today, then, take a general and final farewell of all creatures, and rejoice when of their own accord they turn their backs upon you; for God permits this to help your weakness. For my part, I am delighted at what has happened, and at the little regard that has been shown to you. This manifestation has undoubtedly been as salutary for you as it has been humiliating. Oh, were you able slowly to grow to love this abjection, what progress would you not make!

Jean-Pierre de Caussade

13. *Interior Difficulties*

Consolations and sensible desires are only means for training the will and forming permanent habits. As soon as the will is fixed, consolations and sensible enthusiasm become mere luxuries and we can wait for them with the more patience.

*

We are never so near God as when we have to get on as well as we can without the consolation of feeling His presence. It is not when the child is with his mother that she is most anxious for his welfare. It is when the child thinks he is alone that his mother is most compassionate and thinks of him most tenderly. It is the same with God and ourselves.

*

You ask me, "Why does God do this?" Because what matters most to Him is not that He should do the work Himself; that would and always will be easy for Him. His real desire is to make us do something. By concealing Himself, He can often persuade us to go on by ourselves and to exert more real virtue. But does this prove that He does not love us? Quite the contrary.

When He does not allow you to be aware of His presence for a long time, for longer than you feel you can bear it, it is because He relies on you. And if He does rely on you, it is because He knows He can do so. . . .

Be at peace then, and simply remember not to allow yourself to be distracted by things which merely hover in the back of your mind. . . .

Do not worry about your feelings, but act as if you had those which you would like to have. This is not done by making a mental effort, nor by seeking to feel that which you do not feel; but by simply doing without the feeling you have not got and behaving exactly as if you had it. When you realize that lack of feeling does not hinder reality, you will no longer put your trust in your own thoughts, but in that which our Lord makes you do. We are very slow in realizing this, but we must do so. Come now! have a little of that tranquil fearlessness which makes for good, without so much thought and scrupulousness. Behave just as naturally as if you were coming downstairs!

*

We must not consider that which comes from our natural impulses as being part of our real selves. We are not responsible for our feelings but for our decisions. What does it matter if our sensible nature feels upset? If we act rightly, then all is well. You would probably rather not experience those perpetual contradictions in yourself of which St Paul also complained. But you will remember that our Lord did not agree with him and left him as he was. This is what St Paul meant when he said "Unhappy man that I am! The good that I would I do not and the evil that I would not, that I do!"

In other words, we have not the characters we should like to have and we have those we should like not to have. What are we to do?

Instead of chasing after them, we must simply do without them and be satisfied with acting rightly, without wanting to feel inclined to such action.

The root of many of your troubles is the desire to have only good inclinations. That is neither necessary nor possible. In countless ways we shall always feel ourselves to be wicked, unstable and unreasonable. We must realize that this is our nature and not our real personality; not our true, deliberate and voluntary desire: not the goal of our efforts.

*

The best thing is not so much to see our Lord do away with our difficulties as to see Him sustain us through them. If we were without difficulties might we not think that they would perhaps return and destroy our serenity?

Instead of which, when we realize to what a degree our Lord always gets us out of our difficulties, in spite of our anxieties, weaknesses and failings, then we begin to acquire assurance and serenity even in the midst of our troubles. Thus the difficulty loses its sting and venom; it does not pierce our soul so deeply because we know that our Lord always opens some ways of escape, probably an unexpected one, by which He rescues us from the extreme danger we feared.

Therefore when you say, "I have difficulties, either within or without", you are doubtless looking on the black side of things. Yet it is really all to the good, in that it forces you to see that you are carrying on all the same, and that in consequence Our Lord is ultimately helping you to cross the torrent. . . .

Our Lord is with us in all our troubles and always gives us sufficient help to carry us through.

Smile and even laugh at yourself when you feel all this inner hubbub going on in you. It is the childish language of nature; plaintive, fearful, unreasonable; we always have it with us. It is a splendid habit to laugh inwardly at yourself. It is the best way of regaining your good humour and of finding God without further anxiety.

*

What you need to realize once and for all is that a good state of soul can, in this world, go hand in hand with a feeling of deep inward disharmony. This feeling is nothing more than an accurate recognition of the true state of human life, which is not a state of triumph and splendour but of confusion and cloudiness. . . .

Our Lord acts as do alpine guides. We are roped to Him with a rope which He has Himself made fast; and while He steadily follows the rough tracks by which He wishes to lead us, we seem to be more often on the ground than on our feet. We appear to be suspended over crevasses which do not however engulf us. We go on through the mist and the icy cloud; the path is strange rather than picturesque. But all this does not prevent us from reaching the summits.

That is the true picture of our route and of our progress. From the time we think we are going to find the main route, we worry about not being on it already. But as soon as we realize, like the Swiss, that we are on the native tracks of the country, we instinctively adapt ourselves and are no more troubled by them than an alpine shepherd who goes up and down them every day.

*

Do not be distressed by lack of fervour and consolations. These will come in their own time and their own way. Our Lord wants you to become mature, and maturity needs these periods of obscurity, of disillusionment and boredom. Maturity comes when we have at last realized that we must love our Lord simply and freely in spite of our own horrible unworthiness and of the unworthiness of nearly everything around us. Then a new and lasting incarnation of our Lord takes place in our souls, as it were. He begins to live a new life within us in the very midst of the misery of the world.

That is why the greatest saints have always shown the perfect combination of nearness to our Lord on the one hand, and a deep sense of their own unworthiness and weakness on the other. We should like to love our Lord perfectly; but the only really perfect way is to love Him in a simple, human way. I assure you that it is a very excellent way and, in the eyes of the angels, a most perfect and touching sight.

They see our Lord loved by men, who do not for that reason cease to be men, and they see our Lord loving men who are nevertheless nothing but men. Is there anything on earth more beautiful than that?

Abbé de Tourville

14. Discouragement

My dear Sister,

Just now you are the victim of one of the most dangerous temptations that can assail a well-intentioned soul – the temptation of discouragement. I adjure you to offer every resistance in your power. Trust in God, and be sure that He will complete the work He has begun in you. Your vain fears for the future come from the devil. Think only of the present; leave the future to Providence. A well-employed present assures the future. At all times and in all places strive to cleave and conform to all God's wishes even in the smallest matter; for virtue and perfection consist wholly of this.

Again, God permits our everyday faults only to humiliate us! If you can profit by them and yet remain trusting and at peace, you will be in a better state than you would if you committed no obvious fault and so flattered your self-love greatly, leaving you in grave danger of self-complacency. Actually you can very easily make use of all your faults to become one degree more humble, and to dig still more deeply within yourself the one foundation of all true holiness. Ought we not to admire and bless the infinite goodness of God who can thus derive our greatest good from our very faults? All we need do is to have no love for them, and humble ourselves gently because of them; after each of our falls to pick ourselves up with tireless persistency, and to go to work peacefully to correct them. Subject yourself to God's will in the work you do, but do not be too eager and restless. Do honestly what you believe you ought to do, and rely on Providence for success, knowing neither care nor anxiety and thus possessing as far as possible a tranquil heart and unshackled mind. Be faithful in this practice and you shall dwell in peace even in the midst of perplexity; while the involuntary troubles you may encounter will serve only to increase the merit of the fundamental compliance of your will with God's. May He be blessed for all things and in all things, now and for ever.

Jean-Pierre de Caussade

15. *Spiritual Darkness*

My dear Sister and dear daughter in our Lord,
God's peace be with you now and always!

I realize from what you have told me that you are walking in spiritual darkness. Yet I by no means share the anxiety this state causes you. This way is usual enough in persons of your sex; while there is no doubt that it is the safer in being the less exposed to the vain complacency of self-love or the deception of vanity. This very darkness, therefore, is one of God's graces; for in this life the best means of going to God is to walk by naked faith which is always obscure. Despite this obscurity, you can understand enough about it and can give details enough of it to make it sufficiently plain to any moderately experienced director. So much for what I think of your state in general. Now to deal with difficulties in detail.

1. You say that you cannot pray. Experience has taught me that every person of goodwill who talks in this fashion can pray better than most, since their prayer is simple and humble and in its simplicity escapes being mere formal thought. This kind of prayer involves dwelling in God's presence in faith with a secret and persistent desire to receive His grace according to our needs. Since God sees all our desires, this is the supreme prayer. For, to quote St Augustine, perpetual desire is perpetual prayer. In prayer let your guide be simplicity. Of this you cannot have too much, for God loves to see us like little children before Him.

2. As for holy communion, your growing hunger for the divine fare and the strength it imparts to you are strong reasons for going to it frequently. Give up your fears, then, taking comfort from the assurance I give you.

3. Indifference to all earthly matters and detachment from relatives even are greater graces than you realize. Detachment from self by ceasing all interior self-examination is your one remaining need. Prayer and frequent union with Jesus Christ will complete the work by slow degrees, provided your work is done in forgetfulness of self and remembrance only of God, to whom you must abandon all your interests, spiritual no less than temporal.

4. Whoever said that God asks of you only submission and resignation was right indeed. In these, my dear daughter, utter perfection is to be found – search for it elsewhere is so much error and illusion. A spiritual person having some inclination to the interior life has, properly speaking, but one thing to do: to be submissive and steadfast of heart in every conceivable situation, exterior or interior, in which God chooses to set her. For example: should you be ill: since God wishes it, wish it also as He wishes it and for as long as He wishes it. – But that may possibly leave me incapable of doing any work or service for the community, you may object. – Very well! once more let your attitude be: I accept in advance not only the pain I suffer but the holy abjection and humiliation that go with it. Or – another objection – in that state I may possibly tend to pamper myself somewhat, not making all the effort I could and should. Is this too God's will, assuming I have consulted my superior and my confessor and have followed their instructions blindly? Yes; again say simply: I wish it.

Let us, then, live in peace by complying with every divine desire – in that interior peace in which God Himself lives and works. This, my Sister, is a sure and exalted way. Follow it faithfully, rejecting every antagonistic thought and idea as a suggestion of the devil, the least of whose aims is to spoil that interior peace in which is the soul's chief good and the firm foundation of the spiritual life.

5. You have been guilty of grave imprudence and

definite disobedience in risking a three months' bout of fever. You can be quite sure that a refusal to eat meat on such occasions is stubbornness and not virtue – a mere obstinate clinging to your own will and judgement under a pretext of piety. Most devout and spiritually minded women are to be pitied in such circumstances, though to put up with them requires much patience. At times their illusion is so blind and so fantastic that an angel from heaven could scarcely rid them of it. Be submissively attentive in all things, and in all things show an endurance that is at once sweet, peaceful and patient. Let this be your spirit in performing God's will and so serve your own greatest good.

6. They have been well advised to forbid you to give way to your wish to change your work and to petition for this. I too most emphatically forbid it. So take good care not to oppose God's decree. – But your health is not good enough, you may say. – God can easily give you health. – You have not the necessary talent. – It is always within God's power to provide you with sufficient. Already He has supplied your main need – distrust of yourself in this matter. The one essential is to recognize and be conscious of your own incapacity; for then you will rely only on God; you will appeal to Him in all circumstances, you will attribute nothing to yourself and everything to God; while His blessings alone will turn all things to your increasing advantage. In a word, live in peace and trust in the all-good God, placing as little reliance on yourself as you wish. Be always humbly aware of your own weakness, incapacity and stupidity: these are precisely the tools of which it pleases God to make use that His glory may be made the more strikingly evident.

7. A lack of perception in regard to the truths of religion is in some souls no bad sign. Often it is merely evidence that God means to lead them by the surest way of all – that of simple unadorned faith unaccompanied by the

knowledge and delights He gives when it pleases Him. In the ways of God effort and strife are required only in regard to sin; in all things else peace and tranquillity are the essentials. When acts have been beyond your power, say to yourself: In God's sight all has been accomplished, since God, who is master, has seen my desire, and will give me the ability to act when it is His pleasure. His blessed will shall always be my law. I am in this world only to do this; in this I possess a rich treasure. Let God give others as much as He wishes of wisdom, talents, graces, gifts and conscious spiritual delights . . . my one desire is to be rich only in obedience to His will.

There, my dear daughter, you have your way. Follow it unfalteringly in peace, trust and complete self-surrender. So shall all be well with you and your safety assured.

8. The greatest need you have to further your spiritual advancement is peacefully to endure all God wishes or allows to happen to you, neither complaining nor seeking comfort from your fellow human creatures, nor wasting your energies in futile conversation nor encouraging yourself in frivolous thoughts and vain plans for the future. All these leave you empty of God, and prevent grace from working in you. So be careful.

9. This is what you must do to help yourself concentrate upon God more easily and uninterruptedly in accordance with your desires and needs: (1) find your delight in silence and solitude since these do much for recollection and the interior spirit; (2) read only enduringly worthwhile and thoroughly pious books, and by pausing frequently endeavour to savour rather than to understand or retain what you have read; (3) during the day direct frequent and fervent aspirations to God in regard to whatever may befall – difficulties, temptations, aversions, weariness, contradictions, bitterness of heart and the rest.

10. The prayers you offer God for detachment from all

things are inspired by grace. Persist in them, sure that sooner or later they will be granted. It is fitting that we should wait for God who for so long has waited for us; while the great graces we ask of Him deserve to be desired and waited for with patience and perseverance.

Jean-Pierre de Caussade
to Sister Marie-Thérèse de Vioménil

16. *Inner Confusion*

30 May 1948

Your interesting letter, written with feeling, arrived in good time and I read it with love. Thanks be to our Lord Jesus Christ that in His mercy He has freed you from the heaviness of your inner confusion. This help was according to your faith and not from me a sinner, all tangled in sins. It is good that you ran to God for help at your moments of sorrow, because our soul is created in the image and likeness of God and therefore it is only in God that we can receive help and comfort at such moments.

Know that we cannot go through life without sorrows. The Lord said: "In the world you have tribulation" (John 16:33). If there had been no tribulation, there would have been no salvation, say the Holy Fathers. The Lord chose the holy prophets and apostles to preach, but He did not free them from difficulties, and our Lord Jesus Christ, perfect God and perfect man (without sin) lived a sorrowful life on earth. At the hands of man, whom He created, He suffered reproach, abuse, scorn, ridicule, blows, even shameful death by crucifixion. I advise you not to be dejected. Endure, pray and try to be "wise as a serpent and guileless as a dove" (Matthew 10:16). If you

145

turn to God, He in His mercy will give you wisdom and the meekness of a dove.

Here is my advice to your husband: let him make a firmer decision in his heart not to drink any more and let him pray to God for help, for the Lord hears every man; let him have no doubt about this. Our efforts alone without God's help are weak. Alcohol always flatters and cheats: you start drinking for joy, and the result is sickness of soul, languor and physical illness; I know this from experience. The Lord help him to get free from alcohol. Let him stop drinking and he will feel good, a thousand times as good.

I advise you not to contemplate monastic life. The Lord will lead you to eternal life through married life in the world. Learn to live for Christ in your family life. The Lord sees your good intention and will save you in your family life – have no doubt of this. St Makarios the Great gives the example of two women who were pleasing to God and reached perfection in the spiritual life and were even higher than the recluses. They wanted to spend their lives in monasteries, but for some reasons they had husbands. The Lord, seeing their will to serve God in a monastery, helped them to be saved while living a family life. At the present time life in monasteries is not as you picture it, and with your inexperience of spiritual life you might only be led astray by monastic life.

A few days ago I went on foot to the convent fourteen kilometres from us. I stayed there overnight, observed their life and ways, the enormous amount of work, the scanty food. The Lord help them, they have already become hardened to that life, but newcomers to the convent could hardly endure it.

Our brotherhood is getting smaller; perhaps death is already standing behind the writer of these lines and will soon cut down my life. Lord, have mercy on me, a sinner, and by the ways which Thou knowest deliver me from eternal torment. Amen!

Staretz John

6

The Rhythm of Everyday Life

1. Interior Vicissitudes

My dear Sister,

The various states which you have described to me in your letter are merely the interior vicissitudes to which we are all liable. The alternation of light and darkness, of consolations and desolations, are as useful – are as indispensable, I would say – in the growing and the ripening of virtues in our souls as changes in the weather if crops are to grow and ripen in our fields. Learn, then, to resign yourself to them, and to accept ordeals no less lovingly than consolations. For even the most sorrowful of these ordeals, whether they come from God's justice or His mercy, are equally just, blessed, adorable, lovable and beneficial. Often His justice and mercy join in sending them; but on this earth the operation of His justice is never wholly divided from His mercy. I am delighted that a perception of your wretchedness and your weaknesses and a consciousness of your nothingness are your normal preoccupation during prayer. It is thus that you gradually acquire complete distrust of self and utter trust in God. Thus, too, you are firmly established in that interior humility which is the enduring foundation of the spiritual edifice and the chief source of God's graces to the soul.

You must be neither surprised nor grieved at the destruction your self-love fears: if it were free of this fear it would not be self-love. Only souls already greatly detached from self long for this utter death and, far from fearing it, desire and demand it unceasingly of God. In your case you will have done enough if you endure patiently and peacefully the various stages which bring it about.

149

It often happens that during the day one is aware of inclinations towards God or divine things, and yet this inclination is lacking at prayers. God ordains this to teach us that He is the absolute master of His gifts and His graces, and that He awards them to whom He pleases and when He pleases. Receiving these when we expect them least, and later finding ourselves disappointed in our expectancy, we can no longer argue that they are the reward of our spiritual state, or of the work we do. This is as God designs. For though He be lavish of His gifts, He claims to reserve all their glory to Himself; while He would be obliged to take them back from us, did He see us appropriate any of that glory by being vainly self-complacent.

Jean-Pierre de Caussade

2. *Patience and Magnanimity*

19 August 1900

. . . years ago, Duchesne said to me, and I have so often found him right, in the lives of my various friends and my own:

Work away in utter sincerity and open-mindedness; lead as deep and devoted a spiritual life as you can; renounce from the first and every day, every hope and wish for more than toleration; and then, with those three activities and dispositions, trust and wait with indomitable patience and humility, to be tolerated and excused. You will find that if only you have patience and magnanimity enough to wait so long, and to work so hard, and to put up with apparently small result – *that* result will not fail you: you will be put up with, not more, not one inch more: but *that* much you *will* achieve.

Baron Friedrich von Hügel
to George Tyrrell

3. *Patience in the Spiritual Life*

6 October 1919

I want to write now, also, because, since you cannot come just now (very naturally, though I am truly sorry), I should like to make some remarks upon quite a number of practical points or questions raised by you since last I wrote.

As to the practical points.

Much frequentation of the Cathedral. [his niece was now living in Salisbury.] You know well, how greatly I love this for you. Yet here is one warning I would give you, and would beg you to bear in mind. *Do not overdo it*; I mean, do not take your utter fill, while the attraction is thus strong. If we want our fervour to last, we must practise moderation even in our prayer, even in our Quiet. And certainly it is perseverance in the spiritual life, on and on, across the years and the changes of our moods and trials, health and environment: it is this that supremely matters. And you will add greatly to the probabilities of such perseverance, if you will get into the way (after having settled upon the amount of time that will be wise for you to give to the cathedral, or your prayer of quiet in general) of keeping a little even beyond this time, when you are dry; and a little short of this time, when you are in consolation. You see why, don't you? Already the Stoics had the grand double rule: *abstine et sustine*: "abstain and sustain": i.e., moderate thyself in things attractive and consoling; persevere, hold out, in things repulsive and desolating. There is nothing God loves better, or rewards more richly, than such double self-conquest as this! Whereas all those who heedlessly take their glut of pleasant things, however sacred these things may be, are in grave danger of soon outliving their fervour, even if they do not become permanently disgusted.

Baron Friedrich von Hügel
to his Niece

4. The Rhythm of Life

30 September 1591

There is in this world a continual interchange of pleasing and afflicting accidents, still keeping their succession of times, and overtaking each other in their several courses. No picture can be all drawn of the brightest colours, nor a harmony consorted only of trebles; shadows are needful in expressing of proportions, and the bass is a principal part in perfect music: the condition of our exile here alloweth no unmingled joy; our whole life is tempered between sweet and sour, and we must all look for a mixture of both. The wise so wist, prepared both for the better and the worse; accepting the one, if it come, with liking, and bearing the other without impatience, being so much masters of every turn of fortune, that none shall work them to excess. The dwarf groweth not on the highest hill, nor doth the tall man lose his height in the lowest valley. And as a base mind, though most at ease, will be dejected, so a resolute virtue is most impregnable in the deepest distress.

They evermore most perfectly enjoy their comforts, who least fear their contraries; for a desire to enjoy carrieth with it a fear to lose, and both desire and fear are enemies to quiet possession, making men less owners of God's benefits, than tenants at His will. The cause of our troubles is, that our misfortunes happen, either to unwitting or unwilling minds. Foresight preventeth the one, necessity the other: for he taketh away the smart of the present evils that attendeth their coming, and is not dismayed by any cross, that is armed against all.

Where necessity worketh without our consent, the effect should never greatly afflict us; grief being bootless where it cannot help; needless where there was no fault. God casteth the dice, and giveth us our chance; the most that we can do is to take the point that the cast will afford us, not grudging so much that it is no better, as comforting ourselves that it is no worse. If men were to lay all their evils together, to be afterwards divided by equal portions amongst them, most men would rather take what they brought than stand to the division; yet such is the partial judgement of self-love, that every man judgeth his self-misery too great, fearing he shall find some circumstance to increase it and make it intolerable: thus by thought he aggravates the evil.

When Moses threw his rod from him it became a serpent, ready to sting, and affrighted him so much as to make him fly; but being quietly taken up, it was a rod again, serviceable for his use and no way hurtful. The cross of Christ and the rod of every tribulation, seemeth to threaten stinging and terror to those who shun and eschew it, but they that mildly take it up and embrace it with patience may say with David, *thy rod and thy staff have been my comfort.* In this, affliction resembleth the crocodile: fly, it pursueth and frighteth; follow, it flieth and feareth; a shame to the constant, a tyrant to the timorous.

153

Hold not your eyes always upon your hardest haps; there are fairer parts in your body than scars. Let God strip you to the skin, yea to the soul, so He stay with you Himself: let His reproach be your honour, His poverty your riches, and He in lieu of all other friends. Think Him enough for this world that must be your possession for a whole eternity.

St Robert Southwell
to his friend, Thomas Howard

5. The Providence of God

My dear Daughter,

What a consolation for you that it is God Himself who has made you superioress, since you are such by the ordinary ways! Wherefore His Providence is under obligation to you, on account of its being the disposer of things, to hold you with its hand, that you may do well what it calls you to. Be sure of this, my dear daughter; you must walk with good confidence under the guidance of this good God, and not except yourself from that general rule that *God who has begun in you a good work will perfect it* (Philippians 1:6), according to His wisdom, provided that we are faithful and humble.

But, *here now, it is required amongst the dispensers that one be found faithful* (1 Corinthians 4:2); and I tell you that you will be faithful if you are humble. But shall I be humble? Yes, if you will it. But I will it. You are it then. But I feel distinctly that I am not. So much the better, for this serves to make it more certain. It behoves not to subtilize so much, but to walk simply; and as He has charged you with these souls, charge Him with yours, that He may carry it all Himself, both you and your charge on you. His heart is large, and He wants yours to have a place there. Rest yourself then on Him; and when you commit faults or defects do not distress yourself, but after having humbled yourself before God, call to mind that *God's power is made perfect in infirmity.*

In a word, my dear daughter, it is necessary that your humility be courageous and brave in the confidence which you must have in the goodness of Him who has put you in office; and to cut right off those many doublings which human prudence under the name of humility is accustomed to make on such occasions, remember that Our Lord does not will us to ask our annual bread, or monthly, or weekly, but daily. Try to do well today, without thinking of next day; then next day try to do the same, and not think of all you will do during the whole time of your office; but go from day to day fulfilling your charge, without increasing your solicitude; since your heavenly Father, who has care today, will have care tomorrow and after tomorrow, of your guidance, in proportion as, knowing your infirmity, you hope only in His Providence.

It seems to me, my dear daughter, that I act with great confidence indeed in thus speaking to you, as if I did not know that you know all this better than I do: but it matters not, for it makes more impression when a friendly heart says it to us. I am your, &c.

St Francis de Sales
to a Carmelite Superioress

6. *Let Be!*

A.D. 404

To grieve to excess over the failings for which we must render an account is neither safe nor necessary. It is more likely to be damaging or even destructive. Still worse is it then and perfectly useless to wear oneself out grieving over others' misdeeds. Above all, it is playing into the hands of the devil, and harmful to the soul.

To illustrate my point, I shall tell you an old story. A certain man of Corinth had received the benefit of the holy waters, was purified through the initiation of baptism, had been a partaker at the tremendous rites of the holy table, and in a word, was a sharer of all the mysteries which are ours. Many say that he held the position of teacher. After his holy initiation and all the inestimable benefits to which he had been admitted, and in spite of holding an important position in the Church, he fell into most grievous sin. Looking upon his father's wife with lustful eyes, he did not stop at desire but translated his unbridled will into deed. This brazen act passed beyond fornication and even adultery; it was much worse.

Blessed Paul heard about it, and being at a loss for a suitable and sufficiently grave term for this sin, made the magnitude of the crime clear by another means. *In a word*, he says, *it is heard that there is fornication among you, and such fornication as is not mentioned even among the heathen.* In an effort to emphasize the enormity of such a crime, he does not say, "such as is not perpetrated", but *such as is not mentioned.*

Accordingly, he hands him over to the devil, cuts him off

156

from the whole Church, and allows nobody to partake with him at the common table. It is not right, he declares, even to eat together with such a person, and peremptorily orders that the severest penalty be inflicted upon him; he makes use of Satan as the instrument of vengeance to punish the man's flesh.

And yet he who cuts the offender off from the Church, and refuses to let anyone eat at the same table with him, who orders all to grieve on his account, he who drives him away from all directions as though he were a real plague spot, who has shut him out from every house, handed him over to Satan, and demanded so heavy a penalty for him, this very Paul, when he sees that the man is contrite and repentant for the sins he has committed, and that his deeds prove that he truly has turned over a new leaf, completely reverses his policy. He now orders the same people to whom he had issued these instructions, to adopt the very opposite line of conduct. He who had said: "Cut him off, turn him away, grieve over him, and let the devil seize him", now says – what? *Confirm your charity towards him, lest such a one be swallowed up with overmuch sorrow, and we should be overreached by Satan. For we are not ignorant of his devices.*

Cannot you see that the tendency to grieve beyond measure comes from the devil and is the work of his cunning? Through urging to excess, he converts the healing medicine into a noxious poison, and whenever he falls into excess, a man hands himself over to the devil. That explains why Paul says, *lest we be overreached by Satan.* His words amount to this: "This sheep was covered with a terrible disease; he was set apart from the flock and cut off from the Church, but he has corrected the evil and has become the good sheep that he was before. Such is the power of repentance. Let us welcome him wholeheartedly, let us receive him with outstretched hands, let us embrace him and clasp him to our breasts, let us make him one of us. For if we will not, we give the devil the advantage. Through our carelessness he seizes upon, not what is his own but him who had become ours; he submerges him in an excess of grief, and makes him his own for the future." Therefore St Paul goes on to say: *For we are not ignorant of his designs*; we know well enough how often, when plans for helping someone go awry, he makes use of them to trip up the unwary.

Well now, Paul does not allow a man who has himself fallen into sin – and such a sin! – to indulge in too great a grief, but rather encourages him, urges him on, and busies himself in doing all he can to remove the weight of his despondency. He points out that immoderation is inspired by Satan, and marks a gain for the devil – is in fact a proof of his villainy and the fruit of his wicked designs. How then can it be anything but the greatest folly and madness where other people's sins and their final reckoning are in question, so to grieve and afflict the soul as to involve oneself in a cloud of melancholy culminating in turmoil, confusion, and unbearable agony of mind?

St John Chrysostom
to Olympias

7. *On a Difficult and Contrary Nature*

1899

I have so long now got to see in myself a certain peculiarity, which the Hügel papers have proved to me to be inherited, and traces of which (in varying forms and degrees) I think are in all three children too, though least in you, I fancy. It is a peculiarity which I was long in seeing in myself, and which will give me *arms*-full, *cart*-loads full of fight and work, as long as I live. It is this. There is, on the one hand, a very real degree of originality, a very genuine requirement of a large liberty, of much initiative and great activity, this is good and should get its food and scope. There is, on the other hand, a strong tendency to fall out of the ranks; to break away from the *corporate*, the belonging, as a part, to any one body as a whole: to be difficult and contrary; to be violent and obstinate; to fret when I cannot get my way; not ever, fully and frankly to endorse and deliberately, freely *will* those subjections and limitations, those docilities and obedience with which life is so mercifully full. And it took me long before I saw plainly that *this second tendency* is weak and foolish, *is the deadly enemy of the first*; and that I could only be really true and strong, really manly and Christian, inasmuch as I trained myself to love and will, to insert right into my heart, to take up as it were into my very blood and system, the idea and the fact of all such limitations, dependences, obediences, docilities, as God has surrounded and really saved me with.

I do not know to what degree this same point applies to you; but it is sure to apply in *some* degree, if only because you are a human being and young; probably also because you are a Hügel, and in part a daughter of our day which, of course, has its special weaknesses as well as special strengths. And it is a point on which I naturally care to speak out, because it was the keen consciousness within myself both of the need of a large liberty, and the absolute necessity of its being a real docility and true dependence, and the feeling of how easily I (presumably more than any one of my children) would jib and rear against it, not simply in the home, but in the church and everywhere – that made me bring you girls up, so very unhampered, so very freely. Yes, but with it, of course, I had to run the risk for you, that this would be taken not as a *means*, but as an end, not as making docility, and the beautiful attitude of trust and teachableness, of corporate inter-dependence and tendency to agree whenever reasonably possible, more easy, but as superseding or weakening all these priceless virtues. It might too, of course, so easily be taken as a starting-point for going faster in the same direction, whereas it was considered from the first, but as forming into a positive hindrance and danger if pushed further afield. And I have, of course, seen with my own eyes, this danger become actual for a while, though not in your case. Darling daughter, see carefully to it that such danger as you may find in your case, never becomes a reality, never gets broken down under.

I have had to train myself away from all unnecessary discussions, from all too long or too detailed or constant criticism of others. Even so, I often weaken myself by this fault, and I am trying to practise that most strengthening thing: to take, in cases where I am not called upon to judge or help, just the good and true that I can and do see, and to not judge, not criticize the rest. In this way one can more easily keep and strengthen the immensely important habit of looking up to people, feeling oneself their inferiors and learners.

Baron Friedrich von Hügel
to his daughter Hildegard von Hügel

8. *Courage and Humility*

I desire you to be extremely little and low in your own eyes, sweet and yielding as a dove; to love your abjection and practise it faithfully. Employ willingly all the opportunities of this which occur. Be not quick in speaking, but answer with slowness, humbly, sweetly, and say much by keeping silent with modesty and equableness.

Support and greatly excuse your neighbour, with great sweetness of heart.

Do not reflect upon the contradictions which happen to you; do not look at them, but at God in all things, with no exception. Acquiesce in all His orders most simply.

Do all things for God, making or continuing your union by simple turning of your eyes or outflowings of your heart towards Him.

Do not agitate yourself over anything; do all things tranquilly in a spirit of repose; for nothing whatsoever lose your interior peace, even if everything should be turned upside down: for what are all the things of this life compared with peace of the heart?

Recommend everything to God, and keep yourself still and reposeful within the bosom of fatherly Providence.

In all sorts of occurrences be faithfully unchanging in this resolution of remaining in a most simple unity and unique simplicity of adherence to God by a love of the eternal care which divine Providence has over you. When you find your spirit outside of this bring it back gently and very simply.

Remain unvaryingly in most simple unity of spirit without ever clothing yourself with any cares, desires, affections or designs at all, under whatsoever pretexts.

Our Lord loves you, He would have you all His. Have no longer any arms to carry you but His, nor other bosom to rest in but the bosom of His divine Providence. Direct not your eyes elsewhere, nor let your spirit stay save in Him alone.

Keep your will so intimately united to His that there may be nothing between; forget all the rest, troubling yourself about it no more: for God has desired your beauty and simplicity.

Have good courage, and keep yourself very humble, abased before the divine Majesty; desire nothing but the pure love of Our Lord.

Refuse nothing, painful though it may be; clothe yourself with Our Lord crucified; love Him in His sufferings, and make ejaculatory prayers over them.

Do this indeed, my dearest mother, my true daughter: my soul, my spirit blesses you with all its affection; and may Jesus Christ Himself do in us, with us, and through us, and for His own sake, His most holy will. Amen.

I have, thanks to God, my eyes fixed on this eternal Providence, whose decrees shall be for ever the laws of my heart.

St Francis de Sales
to Mother de Chantal

9. *On Anxiety*

18 May 1947

About your anxiety and stumbling I will say this: as long as the ship of our soul is sailing on the sea of life it will always be subject to changes of weather: now rain, now fine weather. Sometimes a storm blows up and it looks as if the boat were about to strike a reef or run aground. It cannot be otherwise in this vale of tears. Only in the life to come will changes cease. When we are subject to passions – I mean those of the soul, such as conceit, vanity, anger, slyness and demonic pride – under the influence of these passions we think that all people are blameworthy and no good. However, we have not been commanded to require love and justice from others, but it is our own duty to fulfil the commandments of love and to be just. But do not be depressed. In times of trouble go deep into Holy Scriptures and the Holy Fathers and into prayer. Then you will experience peace and quiet in your soul. By our own reason, no matter how hard we think, without God's help we cannot be reconciled with ourselves or bring peace to others.

The Lord keep you.

Staretz John

10. *On Facing Physical Suffering*

FOUR LETTERS

1916

I need hardly assure you that your illness – the weakness and pain you are suffering, in their various degrees and kinds of tryingness – that all these things are now very much in my mind and heart. Indeed they remain constantly present before me, even when they have to be in the background of my consciousness.

With our dearest Gertrud we were able, for a considerable time, to hope that God would still give her many a year of life. And you yourself are not yet sixty, or barely that. May God give you yet many a year of life! But quite distinct from the question of the length of her life, was that of the *quality* of it – of the suffering and limitations mingling with, and imposed upon, pretty well all her activities. All these things were a present, indeed a pressing question.

And looking back now, I am grateful for nothing so much as for this – that, given the suffering and trials which God then sent or permitted, He also soon gave her a light, far more vivid and continuous than it used to be, and an evergrowing acceptance and active utilization of it, as to the place, meaning and unique fruitfulness of such suffering, thus met (as it were) halfway, in the mysterious, but most certain, most real scheme of the deepest life and of God.

When we first got to Rome, she was wonderfully plucky and courageous, "grinning and bearing", a dear Stoic. But then gradually she became, in this too, more and more sensitively Christian. The Cross became, not simply a fact, to bear somehow as patiently as we can, but a source and channel of help, of purification, and of humble power – of a permanent deepening, widening, sweetening of the soul.

It was God's holy Will in *her* case that all this growth should promptly be for the other life. But it would, of course, in no way have been less precious had she been allowed to live on here, thus so greatly deepened and expanded, and rendered so far more helpful than ever before, and that for many a year.

I put all this to yourself, as I do to myself, because I have long felt that it is *the apparent sterility of suffering* which adds the final touch of trial to our pains; and that this appearance is *most truly* only an appearance. Not, of course, that suffering, simply of itself, is good or operates good; but that God is more living and real than all suffering and all sin; and that He can, and will, and does give concomitant opportunities and graces and growths to the sufferer, if and when the latter is humble, watchful and prayerful in such utilizations.

How I wish I could help much, very much, to lessen your pains, but – I admit – above all, towards their trans-mutation! You can and will now help us all a hundred times more than when you were in health; suffering can be the noblest of all actions.

Yours affectionately,

F. von Hügel

*Baron Friedrich von Hügel
to a Friend in his last illness*

To the same friend   28 February 1916

How wonderful it is, is it not, that literally only Christianity has taught us the true peace and function of suffering. The Stoics tried the hopeless little game of denying its objective reality, or of declaring it a good in itself (which it never is), and the Pessimists attempted to revel in it, as a food to their melancholy, and as something that can no more be transformed than it can be avoided or explained. But Christ came, and He did not really explain it; He did far more, He met it, willed it, transformed it, and He taught us how to do all this, or rather He Himself does it within us, if we do not hinder the all-healing hands.

Pray for us all, even just in passing, please. In suffering, we are very near to God.

Your affectionate old friend,

Fr. von Hügel

To the same friend   6 March 1916

I have your three letters – all written since I last wrote – all before me; and I want, first of all, to say that you will never, please, take any little delay in answering as the least index of my feelings. I had to toil under much pressure till this last Saturday afternoon – two days ago. And then a chill drove me to bed and to sloppy food till lunch time today, Monday.

But unless I am absolutely prevented by ill-health or work that will not brook any break, I will write to you every Monday late afternoon, unless (or until) you do not find any special help in such frequent letters or for any other reason which you need not ever specify . . .

As to your spiritual question, my dear . . ., as to how you are, not simply, once for all, at the beginning of all this discomfort and pain, to accept and will it; but (as you most rightly feel, a very different thing) how you are to stand it, to keep on accepting it, day by day, even hour by hour, possibly minute by minute (I mean, as to the proximity of pain to pain, and weakness to weakness): let me suggest to you the following. I take it that *this is precisely the most irreplaceable function and grace of suffering*, when it is at all at its fullest, that we cannot, do what we will, cut a decent figure in our own eyes; that it rises, *emphatically*, beyond a stoic exercise. All we can then do (and how dear and darling this poor little "all" is then to God!) is gently to drop, gently to try to drop, all foresight whatsoever; to treat the question how we are going to stand this for a month, or a week, or a day, or even an hour, as a little presumption on our part. We cannot really, of ourselves, "stand" it properly, for half an hour; and God will and does give us His grace to stand it, for as long as ever He chooses, provided we will, according to the intensity of the trial, contract our outlook, to the day, or the hour, or even the minute. God, the essentially timeless, will thus and then help His poor timeful creature to contract time to a point of most fruitful faith and love.

To the same friend   27 March 1916

Of course, I keep your case, and its necessities and possible helps, well in my mind and in my prayers. And since you continue to press me, so gently yet so firmly, to propose to you *whatsoever* I may believe will or might help you to deepen your spiritual life and fully to utilize the suffering that God Himself is now sending you, I will suggest the two following closer practices and self-examinations. I need not say, that they are both intended simply as rough material, or approximate suggestions for your own experimenting and hewing into shape. I do not even want to hear your impressions upon them – it all aims solely at the depth of your heart and conscience to help the fullest awakening and purification that God may call you to. Certain it is, that only such a growing, deepening (even if interiorly painful at first) can and will anchor your soul in a peace which not all the possible hurricanes of pain or oppressions of physical weakness can break you away from, really, at all.

I would then, first, get my imagination and reason into the habit, not simply of looking at, and looking for, sin as an offence against God, but of realizing and picturing it as *always* (except with hardened grave sinners) *chiefly to a shirking of some effort, or loneliness, or pain, etc., attached to a light or commandment as it offered itself to us, or a seeking of some pleasure, relaxation, vanity, etc., attached to the contrary course.* Now the cure – the only cure – for such shirking of right pain, and for such seeking of wrong pleasure, is precisely the recovering (more and more deliberately) of what mean shirking and mean seeking. *Pain* – most real pain, which comes ready to our hand for turning into *right* pain – gets offered us by God. Try more and more *at the moment itself*, without any delay or evasion, without any fixed form, as simply, as spontaneously as possible, to cry out to God, to Christ our Lord, in any way that comes most handy, and the more variously the better. "Oh! Oh! this is real: oh! deign to accept it, as a little real atonement for real sin!" "Oh, help me to move on, from finding pain so real to discovering sin to be far more real." "Oh, may this pang deepen me, may it help to make me real, real – really humble, really loving, really ready to live or die with my soul in Thy hands." . . . And so on, and so on. You could end by such ejaculations costing your *brain* practically nothing. The all-important point is, to make them *at the time* and *with the pain* well mixed up into the prayer . . . Pray for me too, I beg of you.

Your very affectionate friend,

H.

167

7

On Various Sorts and Conditions

1. Bad Behaviour in Others

It is the greatest blessing to witness the bad behaviour of others without contempt, indignation or impatience, and even without worrying. If for some good reason you mention it, watch over your heart and your tongue, so that nothing escapes that God does not approve of. Say nothing except from good motives. Inwardly groan and humbly regret faults which can often slip into such exchanges. From time to time ask God for caution and charity, and then remain untroubled.

Cherish the saintly wish to belong wholly to God. Pray with faith, confidence and submission; above all deeply humbling yourself before God. It is for Him to complete the work He has begun in you. Nothing else will succeed. Many sacrifices must be made before God fills our hearts with the infinite joy of His perfect love. Since our hearts could not exist without love and affection let us pray and long for it. Only God's love enchants, upholds, possesses and converts them. Let us abandon ourselves unreservedly to God. Let us leave all to His benevolent Providence. Think only of walking resolutely in the path of the present, eternally decreed to be the surest way to our predestination. The act continually fulfilling God's will is the best time spent during our life.

Jean-Pierre de Caussade

2. Rules for a Busy Life

Indeed it is not I that am hard to find, it is you! Please to remember this, and don't talk any more about people keeping me like a relic! I dare not disturb you when surrounded by M. de Gramont, and so many others! Seriously, though I am sorry for your difficulties, you greatly need certain free hours to be given to recollection. Try to steal some such, and be sure that such little parings of time will be your best treasures. Above all, try to save your mornings; defend them like a besieged city! make vigorous sallies upon all intruders, clear out the trenches, and then shut yourself up within your keep! Even the afternoon is too long a period to let go by without taking breath.

Recollection is the only cure for your haughtiness, the sharpness of your contemptuous criticism, the sallies of your imagination, your impatience with inferiors, your love of pleasure, and all your other faults. It is an excellent remedy, but it needs frequent repetition. You are like a good watch, which needs constant winding. Resume the books which moved you; they will do so again, and with greater profit than the first time. Bear with yourself, avoiding both self-deception and discouragement. This is a medium rarely attained; people either look complacently on themselves and their good intentions, or they despair utterly. Expect nothing of yourself, but all things of God. Knowledge of our own hopeless, incorrigible weakness, with unreserved confidence in God's power, are the true foundations of all spiritual life. If you have not much time at your own disposal, do not fail to make good use of every moment you have. It does not need long hours to love God, to renew the consciousness of His Presence, to lift up the heart to Him or worship Him, to offer Him all we do or bear. This is the true Kingdom of God within us, which nothing can disturb.

François Fénelon

3. *On being Criticized by Others*

2 October 1619

My very dear Daughter,

Take good care not to fall into any discouragement when you are murmured at or criticized a little. No, my dear daughter; for I assure you that the business of finding fault is very easy, and that of doing better very difficult. There needs but very little ability to find fault, and something to talk about, in those who govern or in their government; and when someone reproves us, or points out to us the imperfections in our conduct, we ought to listen quietly to it all, then lay it before God, and take counsel about it with our assistant sisters; and after that do what is considered best, with a holy confidence that God will bring all to His glory.

Do not be quick to promise; but ask time to make up your mind in matters of any consequence. This is fitting in order to secure the good success of our affairs, and to nourish humility. St Bernard writing to one of my predecessors, Arducius, Bishop of Geneva: "Do all things", he says, "with counsel, but the counsel of a few persons, who are peaceable, wise and good." Do this so sweetly that your inferiors may not take occasion to lose the respect which is due to your office, not to think that you have need of them for governing; modestly let them know, without saying it, that you are acting so to follow the rule of modesty and humility, and what is prescribed by the constitutions. For you see, my dear daughter, it behoves as far as possible to act so that the respect of our inferiors for us may not diminish love, nor love diminish respect.

Do not trouble yourself at being a little governed by that good soul outside; but go on peacefully, either acting according to her advice in things where there lies no danger in contenting her, or acting otherwise when the greater glory of God requires it; and then you must, as cleverly as you can, gain her approval.

If there be some sister who does not show sufficient respect for you, let her know it through one of the others whom you may judge the most suitable for this, not as if from you but as if from this person herself. And in order that your gentleness may in no way resemble timidity or be regarded as such, if you were to see a sister who made a profession of not showing this respect, you would have yourself sweetly to show her, by herself, that she ought to honour your office and work with the rest to preserve in dignity the charge which binds together the whole congregation in one body and one spirit.

Well now, my dear daughter, keep yourself entirely in God, and be humbly courageous in His service, and often recommend to Him my soul, which, with all its affection, cherishes yours most perfectly, and wishes it a thousand thousand benedictions. When I say to you: do not show this letter, I mean, do not show it indiscriminately; for if it be a satisfaction to you to show it to someone, I am very willing. Your very affectionate father and servant, &c.

*

To know when it is required for contracts that the spiritual Father should be present, and when not, depends on the nature of the contracts; for there are some in which it is required and others where it is not, as the Bishop has need of the presence of his Chapter in some contracts, in others not. It is for instructed people to settle this as occasion arises; one cannot lay down a general rule. There is sometimes inconvenience, but one could scarcely remove it without falling into a greater. Whether M. Dutine calls himself spiritual Father or not in contracts neither makes nor mars, for this name can be understood in various ways.

The work *On the Will of God* can be read, except the last book, which, being scarcely intelligible, might be improperly understood by the imagination of readers, who, desiring these unions, would easily imagine that they had them, without as much as knowing what they are. I have known religious women, not of the Visitation, who having read the books of the Mother [St] Teresa, found on their own reckoning that they had as many perfections and spiritual acts as she had, though they were far indeed from it, so greatly does self-love deceive us.

This expression: Our Lord suffers in me such and such things, is altogether extraordinary; and although our Lord has sometimes said that He suffered in the person of His own, to honour them, yet we ought not to speak so advantageously of ourselves. For our Lord only suffers in the person of His faithful friends and servants, and to boast and proclaim ourselves to be such has a little presumption in it; self-love is often very glad to make its account thereby.

When the doctor has to enter the monastery, to see some sick person, it is enough that he have permission in writing at the beginning, and it will last till the end of the illness; the carpenter or mason to the end of the work for which he enters.

Your way is good, my dear daughter, and there is nothing to object to, save that you go considering your steps too much, for fear of falling. You make too much reflection on the movements of your self-love, which are doubtless frequent, but which will never be dangerous so long as, tranquilly not letting yourself be annoyed by their importunity nor alarmed by their multitude, you say No. Walk simply, do not desire repose of spirit too earnestly, and you will have the more of it. Why do you put yourself in trouble? God is good; He sees very well what you are; your inclinations cannot hurt you, bad as they may be, since they are only left to you to exercise your superior will in making a more profitable union with that of God. Keep your eyes uplifted, my dear daughter, by a perfect confidence in the goodness of God. Do not be anxiously solicitous for Him, for he told Martha that He did not wish it, or at least that He was better pleased that there should be no solicitude, not even in doing good.

Do not examine your soul so much about its advancement. Do not want to be so perfect, but in simple earnest live your life in your exercises, and in the actions which come to be done in their time. *Be not solicitous for tomorrow* (Matthew 6:34). As to your way, God who has guided you up to the present, will guide you to the end. Remain in entire peace, in the holy and loving confidence which you ought to have in the sweetness of heavenly Providence.

Ever pray devotedly to our Lord for me, who cease not to wish you the sweetness of His holy love, and in His love that of the blessed dilection of your neighbour, whom this sovereign Majesty loves so much. I picture you to myself high up in the beautiful air, where you regard as from a holy hermitage the world which is below, and see displayed the heaven to which you are called. I assure you, my dear daughter, that I am greatly yours, and my faith tells me that you do well to live entirely in the bosom of divine Providence, outside of which all is but vain and useless affliction. May God be for ever in the midst of your heart. Amen.

St Francis de Sales
to a Superioress of the
Visitation

4. On Charity and Giving Alms

Two Letters

19 January 1879

Now you no doubt take for granted that your already being or your ever coming to be a Christian turns on the working of your own mind, influenced or uninfluenced by the minds and reasonings of others as the case may be, and on that only. You might on reflection expect me to suggest that it also might and ought to turn on something further, in fact on prayer, and that suggestion I believe I did once make. Still under the circumstances it is one which it is not altogether consistent to make or adopt. But I have another counsel open to no objection and yet I think it will be unexpected. I lay great stress on it. It is to give alms. It may be either in money or in other shapes, the objects for which, with your knowledge of several hospitals, can never be wanting. I daresay indeed you do give alms, still I should say give more: I should be bold to say: Give, up to the point of sensible inconvenience. *Fieri non potest ut idem sentiant qui aquam et qui vinum bibant*: the difference of mind and being between the man who finds comfort all round him unbroken unless by constraints which are none of his own seeking and the man who is pinched by his own charity is too great for forecasting, it must be felt: I do not say the difference between being pinched and being at one's ease, that one may easily conceive and most people know, willynilly, by experience, but the difference between paying heavily for a virtue and not paying at all. It changes the whole man, if anything can; not his mind only but the will and everything. For here applies something like the French bishop's question to his clergy whenever one of them came to tell him that he had intellectual difficulties and must withdraw from the exercise of his priestly functions – *What is her name?* in some such way a man may be far from belief in Christ or God or all he should believe, really and truly so; still the question to be asked would be (not *Who is she?*, for that to him is neither here nor there) but *What good have you done?* I am now talking pure Christianity, as you may remember, but also I am talking pure sense, as you must see. Now you may have done much good, but yet it may not be enough: I will say, it is not enough. I say this, you understand, on general grounds; I am not judging from particular knowledge, which I have no means to do and it would be very wrong and indiscreet.

23 January. I feel it is very bold, as it is uncalled for, of me to have written the above. Still, if we care for fine verses how much more for a noble life!

> *Gerard Manley Hopkins*
> *to Robert Bridges*

St Giles's, Oxford, 29 January 1879

I spoke, then, of alms – alms whether in money or in medical or other aid, such as you from the cases you come across at the hospital might know to be called for. And I said "sensible inconvenience"; that is, for instance, you might know of someone needing and deserving an alms to give which would require you in prudence to buy no books till next quarter day or to make some equivalent sacrifice of time. These are sensible inconveniences. And to submit to them you cannot, nevertheless, call the reverse of sensible. But to "derweesh" yourself (please see the Cairo letter in the last *Athenaeum* – or possibly

Academy),[1] that would *not* be sensible and that is what you took me to mean and that is what it would have been supremely senseless of me to mean.

I added something about it needing the experience to know what it feels like to have put oneself out for charity's sake (or one might say for truth's sake, for honour's sake, for chastity's sake, for any virtue's sake). I meant: everybody knows, or if not can guess, how it feels to be short of money, but everybody may not know, and if not cannot well guess, how it feels to be short of money for charity's sake, etc., as above.

All the above appears to me to be put plainly. It reads to me in the blustering bread-and-cheese style. You will ask why I was not as plain at first. Because the blustering bread-and-cheese style is not suited for giving advice, though it may be for defending it. Besides I did not foresee the misunderstanding. What I did fear, and it made me keep the letter back, was that you would be offended at my freedom, indeed that you would not answer at all. Whereas, for which I heartily thank you, you have answered three times.

It is true I also asked you to give me, if you liked, an account of your mind – which would call for, you say, self-examination, and at all events one cannot say what one thinks without thinking. But this and the almsgiving are two independent things mentioned in one letter. No doubt I see a connection, but I do not need you to.

However if I must not only explain what I said but discover what I thought, my thoughts were these – Bridges is all wrong, and it will do no good to reason with him nor even to ask him to pray. Yet there is one thing remains – if he can be got to give alms, of which the scripture says (I

[1] *The Academy*, 25 January 1879, p. 76: Letter from Cairo, Egypt, dated 4 January 1879, signed Greville J. Chester, and describing the ceremonies connected with the so-called "Martyrdom" of Hussein, including the fanatic behaviour of two groups of Derweeshes.

was talking to myself, not you) that they resist sins and that they redeem sins and that they will not let the soul go out into darkness, to give which Daniel advised Nabuchodonosor and Christ the Pharisees, the one a heathen, the other antichristians, and the whole scripture in short so much recommends; of which moreover I have heard so-and-so, whose judgement I would take against any man's on such a point, say that the promise is absolute and that there is for every one a fixed sum at which he will ensure his salvation, though for those who have sinned greatly it may be a very high sum[1] and very distressing to them to give – or keep giving: and not to have the faith is worse than to have sinned deeply, for it is like not being even in the running. Yet I will advise something and it must improve matters and will lead to good. So with hesitation and fear I wrote. And now I hope you see clearly, and when you reply will make your objections, if any, to the practice of almsgiving, not to the use of hairshirts. And I take leave to repeat and you cannot but see, that it is a noble thing and not a miserable something or other to give alms and help the needy and stint ourselves for the sake of the unhappy and deserving. Which I hope will take the bad taste away. And at any rate it is good of you only to misunderstand and be vexed and not to bridle and drop correspondence.

Gerard Manley Hopkins
to Robert Bridges

---

[1] *These two words written above "great one", cancelled.*

5. Counsels to a Student

A.D. 1270 (?)

You have asked me, John, most dear to me in Christ, how you should set about studying in order to build up a rich store of knowledge. This is the advice I give you on the subject.

1. Do not plunge straight into the sea, but rather enter it by way of little streams, because it is wise to work upward from the easier to the more difficult. This, then, is what I would teach you, and you must learn.

2. I would have you slow to speak, and slow to betake yourself to the parlour.

3. Cherish purity of conscience.

4. Never omit your times of prayer.

5. Love to stay in your own cell if you want to gain admission to God's wine-cellar.

6. Show a cheerful face to all.

7. Never pry into other people's business.

8. Do not become over-familiar with anyone, because familiarity breeds contempt and gives pretext for neglecting serious work.

9. Take care not to interfere in the words and actions of outsiders.

10. Do not waste time in useless talking.

11. Be sure to follow in the footsteps of good and holy men.

12. Do not concentrate on the personality of the speaker, but treasure up in your mind anything profitable he may happen to say.

13. See that you thoroughly grasp whatever you read and hear.

14. Check up on doubtful points.

15. And do your best to hoard up whatever you can in that little bookcase of your mind; you want to fill it as full as possible.

16. Do not concern yourself with things beyond your competence.

By following this path, you will throw out leaves and bear serviceable fruit in the vineyard of the Lord of Hosts all the days of your life. If you stick to these counsels, you will reach the goal of your desires. Farewell.

St Thomas Aquinas
to a disciple

6. *Coping with Illness*

12 December 1952

Christ is in our midst!

. . . You write of your illnesses that they are sent by God for your sins.

No, you must not think that way. The Lord's thoughts are unsearchable, and our limited little minds cannot understand why different kinds of sicknesses and sorrows are given by God to different ones of us sinners. But realize that in this vale of tears, this temporal life, we cannot escape them.

The Lord give you wisdom! Don't think of God as a very stern judge and punisher. He is very merciful; He took human flesh and suffered as a man, not for the saints' sake but for sinners like you and me. We must not despair, for there is no sin that exceeds God's compassion. It is always the devil that brings despair; one must not listen to him. Try as far as possible to fulfil the Lord's commandments.

182

Judge no one for anything and you will not be judged. If you watch yourself, you will of course find sins, which will show you that you have no cause to condemn others. And also: "Whatever you do not wish for yourself, do not do it to others either", and other Gospel commandments.

You also write that you used to pray better, but now you do not hear the Lord knocking at your heart. Do not think like that either! Your prayer used to be dreamy and you thought something of yourself, but now you have begun to understand a little – so you can see yourself more truly. The closer a person comes to God, the more sinful he sees himself to be. St Peter Damascene writes: "If a person sees his sins like the sands of the sea, that is a sign of a healthy soul." This is the position of the saints, and they are experienced in the spiritual life. But people want to see themselves as correct in every respect.

Of course it would be good to have a personal talk about the spiritual life, for it is difficult to write in a letter about the subtleties of the spiritual life.

Be thankful to God that in His goodness He freed you from the hatred you felt towards your husband's parents. And in future try never to have hostility towards anyone, for life and death depend on the neighbour.

The holy Apostle Paul lists the degrees of saints, comparing some to the sun, others to the moon, and others to the stars; and there are great differences among the stars (1 Corinthians 15:41). But may you and I be tiny stars if only we can be in the same heaven. And if something does happen because of human weakness, we should not be dejected. Let us be humble, know our weakness and repent. Man's characteristic is to fall, but the devil's is not to repent.

Lord, let Thy mercy be upon us, as our hope is in Thee. Amen!

Staretz John

7. *Low Spirits*

Dear Lady Georgiana,

. . . Nobody has suffered more from low spirits than I have done – so I feel for you.

1st. Live as well as you dare.

2nd. Go into the shower-bath with a small quantity of water at a temperature low enough to give you a slight sensation of cold, 75° or 80°.

3rd. Amusing books.

4th. Short views of human life – not further than dinner or tea.

5th. Be as busy as you can.

6th. See as much as you can of those friends who respect and like you.

7th. And of those acquaintances who amuse you.

8th. Make no secret of low spirits to your friends, but talk of them freely – they are always worse for dignified concealment.

9th. Attend to the effects tea and coffee produce upon you.

10th. Compare your lot with that of other people.

11th. Don't expect too much from human life – a sorry business at the best.

12th. Avoid poetry, dramatic representations (except comedy), music, serious novels, melancholy people, and everything likely to excite feeling or emotion not ending in active benevolence.

13th. *Do good*, and endeavour to please everybody of every degree.

14th. Be as much as you can in the open air without fatigue.

15th. Make the room where you commonly sit, gay and pleasant.

16th. Struggle by little and little against idleness.

17th. Don't be too severe upon yourself, or underrate yourself, but do yourself justice.

18th. Keep good blazing fires.

19th. Be firm and constant in the exercise of rational religion.

20th. Believe me, dear Lady Georgiana . . .

Sydney Smith
to Lady Georgiana Morpeth

8. On Married Life

24 January 1949

I rejoice that you are striving for the one thing needful; try not to quench the spirit. Married life should not trouble you, for it is blessed by God. Neverthless, try to bear each other's burdens and to fulfil the law of Christ. The Lord give you wisdom!

Of course the world makes its own demands: work, bustle and care, it cannot be otherwise. If with all this you keep God in mind – that is enough. The Holy Fathers consider prayer and remembering God as the same thing. If you ever find time it would be good to do a little reading of the gospels and the apostle's letters and to meditate on this temporal vale of tears and on death and the eternal life to come. Lord, have mercy! It is terrifying even to think that there is no end! Even though it is sometimes very hard here, and all of us poor souls groan under the weight of various

185

troubles, still they do change; whereas there, there will be no changes at all.

You write: "I am afraid of my unworthiness and many backslidings." Do not forget that the Lord Jesus Christ took on our flesh and was a perfect man – without sin – not for the righteous, but for sinners. Glory to Thy mercy, O Lord! The Lord knows our weakness and has granted us the healing of repentance. According to the law of spiritual knowledge, the more a man succeeds in the spiritual life, the more sinful he sees himself to be. St Peter Damascene writes: "If a man sees his sins as sands of the sea, this is a sign of a healthy soul." With these feelings there is no room for despair; one's soul is filled with tenderness and love towards all that live on earth. Blessed are such people, those who reach that state. It is God's reward for deepest humility and is called dispassion.

Staretz John

9. *The Ill Behaviour of Others*

Dear Sister,

There is a great grace in witnessing the ill behaviour of others with neither harshness, nor indignation, nor impatience, nor even with annoyance. If for some good reason you comment on it, curb both your emotion and your tongue that nothing displeasing to God escape you. Further, say nothing at all except your motive be good. On all occasions bear yourself with meek humility, and, when alone, regret those faults that tend to creep into such conversations. Beseech God constantly to give you abundance both of charity and circumspection, and so be at peace. Make yours the blessedness of desiring to be wholly God's; in your prayers let there be faith, trust and self-abandonment. Above all abase yourself humbly before His divine Majesty. It is for Him to finish the work He has begun in you: there is none other that can accomplish it. Yet remember that many sacrifices are necessary before God possesses our hearts with His pure love. Let us long for that happiness, let us beg for it unweariedly; let us buy it with unstinted sacrifice; nor count its cost too dear, however high it be. As it is love alone that can keep our hearts alive, so it is only in God's that the heart can find the nourishment to satisfy its hungry need. Let then this divine love come to us; let it possess our hearts; let it uphold them; let it wrap them round; let it transform them into itself! Let us abandon ourselves unreservedly to God; let our thought concern itself only with following the way which God through all eternity has marked out for us and which we now are treading. Argument about predestination can be endless, and such argument merely serves to make our salvation the more remote. This one thing is certain: there is no better means of making the predestination of our salvation sure than the ceaseless performance of God's will in the present.

Jean-Pierre de Caussade
to Sister Marie Thérèse de Vioménil

10. *To a Friend on His Blindness*

I hear sad news of you. You have passed under the sorest trial that perhaps could have been laid on your courage, your hopefulness, your peace.

I trust indeed that there is much to look for yet of recovered power and renewed work, but for the moment there must be anxiety, the bitter strain of disappointment and the rough curb of pain. You are assured of the deep

sympathy of many warm-hearted friends to whom you
have always shown most generous kindness, and I venture
to rank myself among them. We shall remember you often
and anxiously.

It is a tremendous moment when first one is called on to
join the great army of those who suffer.

That vast world of love and pain opens suddenly to
admit us one by one within its fortress.

We are afraid to enter into the land; yet you will, I know,
feel how high is the call. It is a trumpet speaking to us that
cries aloud, "It is your turn! Endure! Play your part! as
they endured before you, so now close up the ranks! Be
patient and strong as they were!"

Since Christ, this world of pain is no accident untoward
or sinister, but a lawful department of life with experiences, interest, adventures, hopes, delights, secrets of
its own. These are all thrown open to us as we press within
the gates – things we could never learn or know or see so
long as we were well.

God help you to walk through this world now opened to
you as through a kingdom, regal and wide, and glorious.

Henry Scott Holland

11. *Talkativeness*

14 November 1955

I read your letter. You confess to being very talkative. The
Holy Fathers said: One person talks all day and it is
accounted as silence, for he speaks for God's sake; another
is silent all day and it is accounted as empty talk. Examine
your own talkativeness and compare it with the advice of
the Holy Fathers!

You write further that you are much occupied with everyday cares, and prayer goes badly. You must finally recognize that you are not a nun and are living in the world. How could you live without cares? You read the Holy Scriptures but do not understand the power of their teaching. For even the Holy Fathers did not live without cares, and their prayer stopped too and they sometimes felt very weak. But they, being experienced in spiritual warfare, did not lose heart in these changes but endured their unpleasant experiences. St John Kolovos was so wrapped in unceasing prayer full of grace that he forgot the baskets that he was to give to the cattle driver; while on his way to fetch them he forgot what he had gone for. When the same holy man was walking with the cattle-driver along the skete path and the driver made him angry, the holy man fled from him. You see, changes happen even in the saints, yet you want everything to go smoothly for you. Remember how I said to you once in our conversation: "It is better to have an uneasy conscience than virtue with vanity."

Here is what the holy men say: "If you are struggling as you should, do not be proud of your fasting. If you get conceited about it, what use is the fast? It is better for a person to eat meat than to be arrogant and exalt himself." St Moses said: "Strength, for a person who desires to acquire virtues, consists in not losing heart when he happens to fall, but in continuing once more on his way. Not to fall is characteristic only of angels." Pedants who are ignorant of the power of the spiritual life do not like such sayings, for all their piety is in outward conduct. It is very regrettable that, in our inexperience in the spiritual life, we stick to the letter, for the letter kills, and the spirit gives life.

The Lord keep you in His mercy.

Staretz John

12. Perfection for the Pretty Woman

Annecy, 3 May 1604

It is impossible to supply you on the spot with all I have promised you, for I have not sufficient free time to put all the material together on the subject you have asked me to explain. I shall treat of it over several letters, and besides making things easier for me, that will give you breathing-space to digest my instructions.

You are filled with a great longing for Christian perfection; that is the noblest longing you could possibly have. Cherish it, increase it day by day. The means of achieving perfection differ according to diversity of vocation, for nuns, widows, and those in the married state are all bound to seek after perfection but not by the same road. Your way, Madam, since you are married, is to live in close union with God and your neighbour and whatever relates to them.

The principal means of union with God must be found in the reception of the sacraments and in prayer. As to the use of the sacraments, you should never allow a month to pass without receiving Holy Communion, and communicate oftener according to the progress you are making in God's service, and the advice of your spiritual directors. Concerning Confession, however, I should strongly advise you to go much more frequently, especially if you have fallen into some fault which troubles your conscience, as so often happens to the beginner in the spiritual life. Nevertheless, if you lack the necessary opportunity to make your confession, contrition and penance will suffice.

In the matter of prayer, you should make it assiduously,

especially meditation to which you are rather well-adapted, I imagine. Every morning then, devote somewhat less than an hour to it either before the daily round, or else before you sup in the evening, but take care never to make it after dinner or supper, because to do so will injure your health. To make it well, you will find it a help to know beforehand the exact subject upon which you are going to meditate, so that from the very beginning of your prayer, you have the matter prepared.

Over and above that, make frequent ejaculatory prayers to our Lord, and do it at all times and wherever you are, keeping your eyes always on God in your heart and your heart in God. Take pleasure in reading Luis of Granada's studies on prayer and meditation; no one can instruct you better than he, nor with such animation. I should like you to allow no day to go by without spending from between half an hour to an hour in reading some spiritual book; that will compensate for a sermon. There you have the chief means of uniting yourself to God.

And now to the ways and means that aid us to establish right relations with our neighbour: they are very many, but I shall mention only a few. We must see our neighbour in God who would have us show him love and consideration. Such is St Paul's advice (Ephesians 6) when he instructs servants to obey God in their masters and their masters in God. We must put this love into practice by showing our neighbour outward marks of kindness; and although at first it may seem to go against the grain, we ought not to give up for all that, because our goodwill and the habit formed by constant repetition will finally conquer the repugnance of our lower nature. We must occupy our prayer and meditation with the problem, since we must first pray for the love of God, and then always petition for that of our neighbour, especially of those to whom we are not humanly attracted.

I advise you to go to the trouble of making an occasional

visit to the hospitals. Comfort the sick, compassionate their ailments, make it clear that the sight of their sufferings affects you, and pray for them in addition to giving them practical help. But in all you do, take scrupulous care never in any way to irritate your husband, your household, or your parents by overmuch church-going, exaggerated seclusion, or neglect of your family duties. Or again, as sometimes happens, don't let it make you censorious of others' conduct, or turn up your nose at conversations which fail to conform to your own lofty standards, for in all such matters charity must rule and enlighten us, so that we comply graciously with our neighbour's wishes in anything that is not contrary to God's law.

You must not only be prayerful and lead a spiritual life, but you must make it congenial to each and every one around you. Now they will admire it, if you make it serviceable and pleasant. The sick will esteem your devotion if it brings them loving consolation; your family, if they realize it makes you more mindful of their well-being, more approachable in a crisis, more gentle in reproof, and so forth; your husband, if he sees that as your spiritual life advances, the more do you smile upon him and prove your love for him by your sweet bearing; your parents and friends, if they note in you a greater generosity, loyalty, and courteous yielding to their wishes so long as the latter do not transgress God's will. In a word, as far as you possibly can, make your piety attractive.

I have written a short pamphlet on perfection in the Christian life, of which I enclose a copy. Take it in good part along with this letter: they both issue from a heart entirely devoted to your spiritual welfare; it desires nothing so ardently as to see God's work perfected in your soul.

I beg you to give me a share in your prayers and Communions, and assure you in return of a lifelong remembrance in mine.

St Francis de Sales
to a Married Woman

13. *The Gift of Sleep*

Avila, December 1577 [?]

... I praise our Lord, who gives your Paternity that tranquillity and the desire to please Him in everything. It is wonderful mercy on His part that He should occasionally grant you illumination in the shape of such great favours. After all, His Majesty will give you help proportionate to your trials; and so, as you are suffering great trials, you will enjoy great favours too. Blessed be His name for ever and ever.

I assure you, my Father, it will be a good thing if your Paternity can sleep. You see, you have a lot of work to do and, until your head gets into a hopeless state, you do not realize how you are overtaxing your strength. And you know how important it is that you should be well. So, for the love of God, look at the thing from another point of view, and stop devoting the hours in which you ought to be asleep either to making plans – however necessary they may be – or to prayer. Please do this out of kindness to me, for often, when the devil sees that someone is very fervent in spirit, he keeps drawing his attention to things which seem of great importance for the service of God, so that if he cannot prevent good being done in one way, he will do so in another.

St Teresa of Avila
to a Carmelite Friar

8

The Vision of God

1. *Sic Transit Gloria Mundi*

1584

Our life is like the print of a cloud in the air, like a mist dissolved in the sun, like a passing shadow, like a flower that soon fadeth, like a dry leaf carried with every wind, like a vapour that soon vanishes out of sight. St Chrysostom calleth it a heavy sleep, fed with false and imaginary dreams; again he calls it a comedy, or rather, in our days, a tragedy, full of transitory shows and disguised passions. St Gregory Nazianzen calleth it a child's game, who buildeth houses of sand on the shore, which the returning wave washeth away; yea, as Pindar saith, it is no more than the shadow of a shade. It passeth away like the wind; it rideth past like a ship in the sea that leaveth no print of passage; like a bird on the air, of whose way there remaineth no remembrance; like an arrow that flieth to the mark, whose track the air suddenly closeth up. Whatsoever we do, sit we, stand we, sleep we, or wake we, our ship, saith St Basil, is always sailing towards our last home. Every day we die, and hourly lose some part of our life; and even while we grow we decrease. We have lost our infancy, our childhood, our youth and all, till this present day; and this very death by minutes is secretly purloining from us. This St Gregory well expresseth, saying, "our living is a passing through life, for our life, with her increase, diminisheth. Future things are always beginning, present things always ending, and things past quite dead and done. No armour resisteth, no threatening prevaileth, no entreaty profiteth against the assault of death." If all other perils and chances spare our life, yet time and age will, in the end, consume it. Better it is, since death is nature's necessary wreck, to follow St Chrysostom's counsel, "let us make that voluntary, which must needs be of necessity; and let us offer to God as a present, what, of due and debt, we are bound to render. What marvel if, when the wind bloweth, the leaf fall; if, when the day appeareth, the night end?" – "Our life", saith the same saint, "was a shadow, and it passed; it was a smoke, and it vanished; it was a bubble, and it was dissolved; it was a spider's web, and it was shaken asunder."

St Robert Southwell
to his fellow Catholics in prison

2. *The Vision of God*

Let us not content ourselves with loving God for the more sensible favours, however elevated, which He has done or may do us.

Such favours, though never so great, cannot bring us so near to Him as faith does in one simple act. Let us seek Him often by faith. He is within us; seek Him elsewhere.

If we leave Him alone, are we not rude, and do we not deserve blame, if we busy ourselves about trifles which do not please and perhaps offend him? It is to be feared these trifles will one day cost us dear.

Let us begin to be devoted to Him in good earnest. Let us cast everything besides out of our hearts. He would possess them alone. Beg this favour of Him. If we do what we can on our part, we shall soon see that change wrought in us which we aspire after.

I cannot thank Him sufficiently for the relief He has vouchsafed you. I hope from His mercy the favour of seeing Him in a few days.[1]

Let us pray for one another.

Brother Lawrence

[1] *Brother Lawrence took to his bed two days later and died within the week.*

3. *The Kingdom of Eternal Bliss*

c. 1160

Let the glorious procession go into the high Jerusalem, the everlasting city of heaven. Christ Himself will be at its head, and all the members of His Body that are gathered together in Him shall follow in His train. There the glorious King shall reign in them, and they in Him. And they shall receive the kingdom of eternal bliss as their inheritance that was prepared for them even before the world was created. We cannot know what that kingdom will be like, and so how can we write about it? But this I know for sure, and I make so bold as to say – that you will lack nothing that you desire, and you will not have anything that you would rather be without. There shall be no weeping nor wailing, no sorrow nor dread, no discord nor envy, no tribulation nor temptation. There will be no such thing as corruption, suspicion or ambition; no such thing as the sickness of old age, death or poverty; no trace of need or weariness or faintness. And where none of these things is to be found, what else may there be but perfect joy and mirth and peace; perfect security, and unmarred love and charity; perfect riches, beauty and rest; health and strength and the perfect sight of God? And in that everlasting and perpetual life what more could you want? God our creator will be clearly seen, known and loved. He will be seen in Himself as He reigns in perfect bliss. He will be seen in His creatures as He governs and rules all things without the least trouble or toil, as He keeps all things unwearyingly, and as He gives Himself to all things in the measure that they can receive Him, without any lessening of His

Godhead. The face of God that the angels desire to gaze upon, shall be seen in all its sweetness, lovableness and desirability. But who may speak of the clearness and brightness of that vision?

There shall we see the Father in the Son, the Son in the Father, and the Holy Ghost in them both. There God our creator will be seen, not as in a mirror or in darkness, but face to face, as the Gospel says. There God will be seen as He is, when the promise that He made in the Gospel is fulfilled: "Who loves Me shall be loved by My Father, and I shall love him and show him My own self." And it is from this clear sight of Him that that blissful knowledge comes of which Christ speaks in the Gospel: "This is eternal life, that they may know Thee, the one true God, and Jesus Christ whom Thou didst send." From this knowledge there springs so great a fervour of blissful desire, so much fullness of love, so much sweetness of charity, that the completeness of bliss may not take away the joyful desire, nor may the desire stand in the way of completeness. And how can we say all this in a few words? Surely, sister, it is in this way: "Eye hath not seen, nor ear heard, what God has made ready for those who love Him."

St Aelred of Rievaulx
to his sister

Acknowledgements

I am grateful to Mr Robin Waterfield and the Amate Press for permission to quote from their edition of the letters of the Abbé de Tourville. I also acknowledge the kind permission of Messrs Darton, Longman and Todd for permission to quote from the following publications, in which they hold the copyright:

Letters from the Desert by Carlo Carretto 1972
An Oratory of the Heart edited by Robert Llewellyn 1980
Christ in our Midst by Father John 1977
The Hermitage Within by A Monk 1980

I would also like to thank Daphne Wright and John Orme Mills O.P. for helpful suggestions, and my editor at Collins, Sarah Hedley, for believing that this collection could interest enough people. I hope she is proved right.

Index of Authors

Smith, Sydney 184
Southwell, St Robert 152, 197

Teresa of Avila, St 193
Tourville, Abbé de 19, 21, 41, 59, 64, 72, 135

Vénard, Blessed Théophane 29